JENSEN INTERCEPTOR

THE COMPLETE STORY

Other Titles in the Crowood AutoClassics Series

JENSEN INTERCEPTOR

THE COMPLETE STORY

John Tipler

The Crowood Press

First published in 1991 by
The Crowood Press Ltd
Ramsbury, Marlborough
Wiltshire SN8 2HR

www.crowood.com

Paperback edition 2004

© The Crowood Press Ltd 1991 and 2004

British Library Cataloguing-in-Publication Data
A catalogue record for this book is available from the British
Library.

ISBN 1 86126 711 8

Picture credits
The majority of the photographs in this book were kindly supplied
by The Motoring Picture Library, Beaulieu. The line drawings on
page 149 and 150 were drawn by Bob Constant.

Typeset by Action Typesetting, Gloucester

Printed and bound in Malaysia by Times Offset (M) Sdn Bhd

Contents

Acknowledgements

When I was but a teenager in rural Essex during the mid-1960s, and obsessed by Italian motor scooters, the scourge of the local country lanes thereabouts was a young-farmer type with a Jensen 541. It was as well to keep out of the way if you saw him about to depart from the pub car-park, especially if Lambretta mounted; only later when I made his acquaintance did I get to ride in the car, and first impressions always endure.

Most striking was the length and attitude of the bonnet under acceleration, the high velocities with which he was able to negotiate the narrow bends, and the smallness of the interior. So this was what grand tourers were all about. A far cry from the family Oxminster, although the 541's straight-six was directly related to the A110's.

After that I always preceived Jensens as being in a different league to me, and I turned to the likes of the MGB and the Lotus Elan for my transports of delight. Therefore it has to be said that my background knowledge of the Jensen marque was somewhat sketchy when I began to write this book, so I am extremely grateful for all the assistance I have had in composing it.

Much in the order in which I contacted them, the list includes Peter Thomas, Tony Wharton, Eric Ward, Albert Mundy, Pat Skidmore, John Taylor, Hugh Wainwright, Lynne Dodd, all at Jensen Motors; Ian Orford; Andrew Edwards of Cropredy Bridge Garage; Steve Mee of Exclusively Jensen; Keith Anderson of the Jensen Owners' Club; and Chris Gill and his colleagues at the National Motor Museum, Beaulieu.

THE JENSEN INTERCEPTOR IN CONTEXT

October 1965	Jensen Motors launch P66 protype and C-V8 FF at Earls Court Show.
April 1966	Kevin Beattie sees Italian stylists.
September 1966	Alan and Richard Jensen retire.
October 1966	Launch of Interceptor and FF at Earls Court.
December 1967	Last Austin Healey 3000 leaves Jensen factory.
June 1968	Norcros sells Jensen Motors to Wm. Brandt's bank, with Carl Duerr as Managing Director.
August 1969	Thousandth Interceptor delivered.
October 1969	Mark II Interceptor, FF II, announced.
April 1970	Kjell Qvale buys Jensen Motors; Duerr replaced by Alfred Vickers.
October 1971	Interceptor Mark III and SP models announced.
March 1972	Jensen Healey introduced at Geneva.
October 1973	Arab-Israeli conflict sparks oil shock. Prices rise 17 per cent.
March 1974	Interceptor Convertible introduced.
December 1974	Four hundred laid off, remaining workers put on short time.
September 1975	Death of Kevin Beattie.
October 1975	Interceptor Coupe introduced.
May 1976	Jensen Motors Limited closed down. Jensen Parts and Service formed.
July 1977	Britcar Holdings wins Subaru franchise.
September 1978	Old Jensen factory sold off.
June 1982	Ian Orford buys Jensen Parts and Service.
October 1983	Mark IV (Series Four) Interceptor introduced at Motorfair.
January 1989	Hugh Wainwright's Unicom Holdings buys Jensen Car Company.
June 1992	The receivers are called in. Jensen Interceptor production finally ends.
January 1998	West Midlands company Creative obtains rights to the Jensen name. Production begins on Merseyside of Jensen S-V8 sports car.
November 1998	Jensen S-V8 launched at NEC Motor Show.
July 2001	Jensen Motors went into receivership.

Introduction

Perhaps a slow, lingering death was preferable to a short, sharp demise, because it allowed what remained of the hard-bitten Jensen workforce to produce a few more Interceptors before the firm finally went under in 1992. It was an achingly slow process. At the end of 1990, when I originally wrote this book, one vehicle was

By 1990, the premises of Jensen Cars Limited was the old parts department, all that remained of the original Kelvin Way factory.

being painstakingly built roughly every six weeks. At the peak of its production, the output was more like twenty-five cars a week, but it started off at something of a trickle because it was more or less a side-line to Jensen Motors' sub-contract work on cars like the Austin-Healey. The Interceptor was always very much hand-built, and in its heyday in the late 1960s and early 1970s, output was akin to that of another quintessential British manu-facturer, Morgan. Jensen Motors Limited was regarded as a proper motor manu-facturer in the 1950s and 1960s, with premises three or four times larger than the factory it occupied latterly.

The Interceptor's history was a turbulent one, for the company passed through a suc-cession of owners and administrators, whose first interest was simply an enthusiasm for the cars. This was fine up to a point, but not necessarily practical. It was the aim of Jensen Car's last owner, Hugh Wainwright, to make the company profitable and secure so they could get on with making cars in quantity again. Sadly, it was not to be.

The Interceptor in its 1966 incarnation is probably Jensen's best-known model. Its predecessors were the technically advanced and stylistically up-to-the-minute 541 and C-VBs, but these too were made in relatively small numbers compared with the Austin-Healeys. When subcontract work for BMC, Rootes Group and Volvo's P1800 terminated, Jensen was in serious trouble, as the Healeys would have to a great extent subsidized and supported production of the Interceptor.

Like the C-V8 before it, the Interceptor's lugubrious character relied to a certain

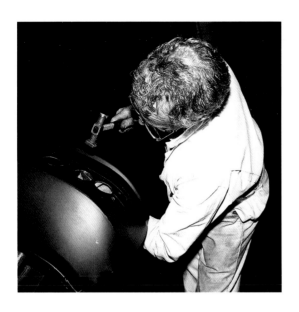

7.2-litre Interceptor. This was virtually contemporary with the launch of the Jensen-Healey sports car which, dogged with problems of reliability concerning its Lotus-derived engine and an over-ambitious production schedule, probably contributed most to the company's downfall. Late in 1975, Jensen Motors Limited closed down.

What had been the former parts department was resurrected from the gloom as Jensen Parts and Service Limited, and by 1983 the Interceptor was back in strictly limited production. During the following decade, however, even in motoring circles and, indeed, in 1990 at a local pub in West Bromwich when I researched this book, the firm was widely supposed to have closed down altogether, or at best perceived as a restoration facility for jaded Jensens.

This was also true, for the principal activity at the Jensen Cars factory during its twilight years was the refurbishing of customers' cars, along with the steady creation of body panels for stock and

extent on its large and, by European standards, thirsty Chrysler power plant. In 1974 following the Yom Kippur war, the first oil shock occurred, turning everybody off gas-guzzlers like the 14mpg (495km/100l)

The prototype Interceptor, pictured in 1968, when it had been re-registered HEA1D; procuring this type of personalized number-plate was more of a game than a status symbol in those days, but Jensen Motors were fortunate in obtaining the first three HEA numbers. Doubtless, the PR advantage of presenting the car with an eye-catching registration was not lost on them.

Launched at Earls Court in October 1968, the Mk I Interceptor design was originally by Touring Superleggera and Vignale, completed by Jensen's Eric Neale.

restoration projects. The single car in-build progressed slowly, as workers found time to add a section of bodywork to the chassis. Every one was a convertible as well. It wasn't a particularly concerted effort, although all employees were enthusiastic about the product. There was an up-beat atmosphere of anticipated change, with the prospect of a substantially revised Interceptor for 1992.

Proprietor Hugh Wainwright was a little like Tony Parkinson of specialist Jaguar restorers Vicarage Cars, who liked the Mk II Jag so much he bought the company. It was hoped – in vain as it turned out – that Jensen's new ownership would fund a trans formation, with new lines, presses, paint and trim shops, so that when revised EU regulations governing motor vehicle manu- facture came out in 1992, a new Jensen Interceptor Mark V could become a reality.

Illustrations for the model showed a car similar in size to the regular Interceptor, but with integral bumpers and front air dam, and running with bigger-diameter road wheels. The effect was to tighten up

Many customers brought their cars back to the factory for maintenance and restoration. Here is a Mark III Convertible waiting its turn in 1990.

The Interceptor was always hand-built. Once the bodyshell was painted, the mechanical components, wiring loom and internals were installed.

the design and make the car more contemporary-looking; head on it appeared reminiscent to the contemporary Aston-Martin Virage.

In those days of joint ventures, when components were traded by manufacturers like Rover and Honda as a matter of course, the Interceptor would not have been out of place. But like all small specialist producers, Jensen always used bought-in mechanical components, and this placed the Interceptor in a different bracket from a luxury tourer such as an Aston-Martin, where all components were designed specifically for a particular model and manufactured in-house. In a world where some can still afford to run high fuel-consumption cars, the Interceptor would still not be out of place.

In the last days of Interceptor construction, there were are a handful of cars still in production whose specification was not dissimilar to what it was when they were introduced some thirty-five years ago: the Porsche 911, the Alfa Romeo Spider, the Morgans; some would have argued for a restored MGB with a new British Heritage shell. The Interceptor

fitted happily amongst them, although admittedly it lacked any major development during its years in the wilderness other than a slightly smaller engine. As with the Morgan, you would be hard pressed to date an Interceptor, unless it was a convertible, in which case it would have to be post-1974.

The Interceptor may have lacked refinement in its drive-train and suspension, compared with rivals like Aston-Martin or Maserati but, conversely, that should have made for better reliability. When in series production, however, it was a trend-setter in one or two significant ways. Not least, the FF model was the first 'mass produced' four-wheel-drive car and the first with anti-lock brakes, and the power steering was as good as any on the market. It remains an excellent long-distance grand-touring classic in which performance is effortless and, given a smooth road surface, provides excellent driving comfort.

Was it worth the lofty £100,000 price tag asked latterly? All said and done, the design dated from 1965, and it was always mechanically unsophisticated, if adequately competent. The answer was 'probably not' when you considered what was available with a far more modern specification. But at a time when it was fashionable, either from a financial or a genuinely enthusiastic point of view, to own a restored or original classic car, which in the case of a Ferrari could cost many times that figure, or virtually the same for a Vicarage E-Type, the Interceptor's price began to look rather less outlandish. Mechanically, a DBS V8 may have been more sophisticated and, like the Bristols, of purer lineage, but you would have had to spend a lot more than Jensen money to get one. Now it's gone for good, and can be bought on the classic market for under £10,000. Remove the rose-tinted glasses, and the Interceptor still has charisma and poise, and is one of the archetypal sixties designs. In the 21st century, surely the main issue with ownership of this rare, limited-production car is affording the fuel bills.

1 The Origins of the Company

As the name suggests, the Jensen family were second generation Danish immigrants, and the Jensen brothers' father was a shipbroker and shipping agent, based in suburban Birmingham at Moseley. Alan Jensen was born in 1906 and, as a boy, he was more inclined towards collecting birds' eggs and dabbling in amateur radio than things mechanical. He began his career in the motor trade as an apprentice with Serk Radiators, where he progressed through most departments before ending up in the drawing office. Born in 1909, Richard Jensen was more interested in cars, and read the journals avidly; he started off as an apprentice at Wolseley.

The home-made car of Alan Jensen's friend Cecil West failed to impress him, but he quickly realized that he and his brother could produce something rather better. So when their father helped them buy a two-year-old Austin Chummy in 1925, they dismantled it and converted it into a boat-tailed, cycle-winged sports roadster. With an eye to corporate styling identity even then, Alan constructed a special radiator, which was similar to the contemporary Sunbeam. Working at Serk Radiators made this task somewhat easier to do after hours. They were given a pair of SU carburettors by Carl Skinner, who founded the company, and soon the car was ready for an outing to the Shelsley Walsh hill-climb.

The Austin 7 Special, 'No. 1', was sold and bought back again, when it underwent further refinements to the body. It was spotted by Arthur Wilde who was chief engineer of the Standard Motor Company. He was particularly impressed by the Jensens' innovations and presentation standards, and asked them to do a similar job on a Standard Nine chassis. The brothers produced just what was wanted, again featuring an appropriately distinctive radiator, and Wilde was delighted. He introduced Alan Jensen to *Autocar* journalist Monty Tombs, who in turn introduced the Jensens to Avon Bodies, a small firm of specialist coachbuilders based at Warwick. Alan was hired to design and build a production roadster, and what they got was a car closely modelled on the Standard, Jensen's 'No. 2', and it became the Avon-Standard two-seater drophead coupe. The firm also made bodies for a variety of small-car chassis, selling for about £80 each, one of which was the Wolseley Hornet.

Richard has left Wolseley and gone to work for Joseph Lucas but, by 1931, the brothers had been invited to work for Birmingham motor trader J.A. Patrick at Edgbaston Garages Ltd. They effectively reorganized his business for him, rationalizing the stores operation and lengthening the opening hours. Soon they had set up a coachbuilding operation, based on the Wolseley Hornet chassis. They became board members, but a row within the Patrick family about the Jensens' status within the firm led to the brothers quitting.

They were swiftly hired by a small firm of coachbuilders at Carters Green, West Bromwich, specializing, not too well, in commercial vehicles. As joint Managing

Directors, the Jensens set about improving the build-quality of the delivery vans and coaches made at W. J. Smith & Sons' workshops. Richard's expertise was on the business side, whilst Alan managed design and production.

Coaches, trucks and vans were the main part of the business, and Alan Jensen was constantly updating production methods and equipment. Later in the decade, the Jensens would collaborate with the Reynolds Tube Company for the building of three extremely dvanced unit-construction aluminium-chassis trucks, known as the JNSN. Meanwhile, by 1934, they had turned their attentions to coach-built sports cars,

and they were in a position to rename the company Jensen Motors Limited, William Smith having retired. Customers for bodies included Standard, Singer, Wolseley and Morris. They were in direct competition with another specialist builder, William Lyons, whose Swallow bodies graced Austins and Wolseleys. The Jensens' Morris conversion retailed at £225 for the finished car, whilst the Swallow undercut them at £215. The Jensen formula was then, as always, to aim for a rather higher market segment than Jaguar.

In 1935, the firm built its very first Jensen. It was to a special order from Hollywood star Clark Gable, and was based on a stock Ford chassis, one of a pair shipped from Detroit,

The first true Jensen was built for Clark Gable; and subsequently twenty replicas of the Hollywood star's Ford V8-powered convertible were produced.

and powered by a 3.6-litre Ford V8. Two identical cars were built, one for Gable, and one for sale, and, ironically, Gable preferred the dark blue car at the dealer's. A big car by British standards, it was not big enough for Gable, and he got himself a Duesenberg. However, there is no better publicity than selling one of your cars to the top heart-throb of the silver screen and, at first, there were many orders for copies of the Jensen. Ford initially refused to supply the necessary components. Jensen friend Lord Brabazon introduced them to Edsel Ford, who visited the Jensen works on a trip to England. He was impressed with the styling and high standards of craftsmanship, and agreed to supply the parts. In all, some twenty copies of Gable's luxurious four-seater tourer, the Jensen-Ford, were made.

The convertible was joined by another Ford-engined Jensen prototype. Known internally as the White Lady, this was a long, low, sleek car with a far more sporting appearance than the Gable car. The box-section chassis was built to Alan Jensen's design by Rubery Owen, and the majority of the components was from the Ford V8.

It was not going to be a big seller, so a more rational direction was taken with the S-Type, which was in effect the first proper

The Jensen S-Type drophead-coupe was introduced in 1936, and was said by The Motor *magazine to 'combine the manners and appearance of a fine town carriage with the performance of the most brazen sports car'.*

The handsome 3.5-litre S-Type of 1936 had a top speed of 89.1 mph (143.4kph), and could travel from 0–60mph (0–100kph) in 19.2 seconds.

On the Jensen stand at the 1938 Earls Court Motor Show; models displayed are open and closed versions of the S-Type, and an H-type with the 4.2-litre straight-eight Nash engine in the foreground.

Jensen production car. It was built in open and closed forms as the saloon, the sports tourer, and the drophead coupe, until 1939. By the mid-1930s, Jensen were establishing a reputation for building relatively inexpensive, good-looking luxury vehicles, clad in distinctive hand-made bodies with an abundance of power. They drew a line somewhere between sporting, luxurious and imposing, whilst all the while being decidedly stylish. Following the S-Type came the H-Type, which had a longer wheelbase and a 4.2-litre straight-eight Nash engine or, alternatively, a 4.3-litre Lincoln V12.

During the Second World War, production was devoted to the construction of service vehicles, including ambulances, fire engines, amphibious Sherman tanks and light trucks. They also made barrage balloon facings, aircraft seats and even bomb cases; some-

During the Second World War, production at Jensen Motors Limited was given over to a variety of military applications, including this armoured car.

body had to. The war years were crucial for Jensen, not for the products they made but for whom they made them: Leonard Lord, Managing Director of Austin provided Jensen with a great deal of their war work, and the liaison was to be reawakened after the war.

TIME FOR THE COMMERCIALS

The brothers' early days at W. J. Smith & Sons gave them an excellent grounding in the production of commercial vehicles and, in 1939, the innovative Jensens collaborated with Reynolds Aluminium to produce three lightweight trucks which were radically different from anything seen previously. Reynolds had a need to transport long sections of aluminium pipe at speed, and contemporary heavy lorries were faced with speed restrictions. The vehicles produced by Jensen had integral chassis-body units, all in light alloy, and combined a length of some 27ft (8m) with an unladen weight of 45cwt (2,286kg), thus successfully undercutting the

The Jensen brothers' background at commercial coachbuilders W.J. Smith & Sons gave them an ideal grounding for the manufacture of coach and commercial vehicle bodies.

One of three trucks with art deco styling built in 1939 for the Reynolds Tube Company for transporting aluminium rods. This was the first of the innovative JNSN lightweight chassis; it was powered by a Ford V8 engine and had a carrying capacity of 5 tons.

Jen-Tugs were a common sight in post-war Britain, and many were exported. Powered by 10bhp Ford and later 13bhp Austin engines, the Jen-Tug was an ideal work-horse for short distance deliveries by organizations like British Railways. Even around the Jensen factory, the Jen-Tug was put to good use, seen below with two Jensen-built A40 Convertibles.

JNSN chassis like this pantechnicon saw service in all walks of life. It was a complex lattice of 14-gauge alloy spars, and the Luton body had a carrying capacity of 1,690cu ft.

speed/weight regulation. Their carrying capacity was 4 tons (4,064kg).

The onset of war was the only thing which halted the development of these fantastic-looking vehicles and, remarkably, they were cheaper to produce than conventional trucks.

General Manager at the time was Colin Riekie, an ex-Daimler man and, in 1939, he instigated the assembly of a small workhorse called the Jen-Tug. This mini-artic prototype served in and around the factory during the war, and was put into production immediately afterwards. The sturdy little Jen-Tugs were available with fourteen different trailer-section options, mostly 13ft (4m) long, and there was even a tipper variant. Initially powered by 1,172cc Ford

engines, and later 1,200cc Austin A40 units, they became a familiar sight performing all kinds of short-haul collection and delivery work.

Putting the experience gained with the Reynolds alloy trucks to good use, Jensen brought out their own range of commercials in 1946. Like the alloy vehicles, they were called JNSNs, with this unmistakable logo stamped into the front panel to act as a radiator grille. The JNSN chassis was a comprehensive crossed and braced network of riveted angle-section alloy girders, and the standard powerplant was the six-cylinder Perkins P6 Aeroflow. One maintenance feature was that an entire engine transplant could be performed in a matter of 3 hours, approximately.

*Jensen's technically advanced lightweight JNSN chassis were used for a
variety of commercial vehicles, such as this early post-war coach. The body is
by Reading & Co. of Portsmouth, and it was used for excursions round the
Isle of Wight.*

The trucks were just as innovative in their
way as the cars, featuring Girling hydraulic
brakes with twin leading shoes. The JNSN
chassis was normally equipped with either a
Luton-type pantechnicon or a flat-bed lorry
back. Production increased to such an extent
that a commercial vehicles plant was built at
Stoke on Trent, transferring to yet another
factory at Kingswinford in 1951, and finally
to Kelvin Way in 1956.

From 1958, the company produced the BMC
1,500cc-powered, front-wheel-drive Tempo,
another commercial vehicle with the em-
phasis on ease of loading. The load-carrying
section could be raised or lowered by hy-
draulics according to the height required by
the operators.

PEACE OFFERING

With hostilities over, Jensen quickly got
back to making car bodies, this time to
supply new clients Invicta and Lea-Francis.
The post-war economic climate was hardly
conducive to selling a great many luxury
cars; Britain seemed doomed to a decade of
stylistic mediocrity, as austerity and
functionalism ruled the economy. Almost
universally, Italy was seen as the leader in
car design, with Pinin Farina, Ghia, Touring
Superleggera, Bertone, Vignale and the rest
of the styling houses setting the trend. Yet
the major British manufacturers studiously
copied largely pre-war American designs,
more or less as they were to continue to do

throughout the next decade. Really only the little firms maintained the free-thinking integrity of their design departments, and only Allard, Aston Martin, Bristol, Jaguar, Jensen, and latecomer Lotus, stand out today. The exception to the rule is that the sports models produced by the big companies like Austin, Triumph and MG were fairly distinctive. Indeed, it has to be said that Donald Healey's new sports car and William Lyons' XK-120 led the way in all-enveloping bodywork in Britain.

Jensen Motors' own post-war offering was the big PW saloon, panelled in alloy over an ash frame, just as the Morgan is made today, and running at first with 3.8-litre Meadows straight-eight engines; but when crankshaft

vibrations proved insoluble, they reverted back to the pre-war Nash unit. The similarity between the PW saloon and the later Austin Sheerline limousine did not go unnoticed. The Jensens were convinced that Leonard Lord and his team had copied the PW prototype seen at the previous year's Motor Show. Lord, of course, denied this, and subsequently offered to provide Austin's 4-litre, six-cylinder Sheerline engines for the PW saloon and Interceptor cabriolet. The only problem then was how to convert the sales brochure from Jensen straight-eight to straight-six. They used stick-on panels.

Austin also went to Jensen for their A40 pick-up trucks, as well as the more significant A40 Sports, introduced in 1950,

The Interceptor shared many stylistic similarities with the A40 Sports; part of the deal for components with Austin involved Jensen designing and building the A40 model. The vent on the bonnet reveals this to be an early Interceptor.

for which Jensen went on to produce 3,500 bodies.

The similarities in styling between the A40 Sports and the first car to bear the Interceptor name, thought up by Lord Strathcarron, were no accident. The Jensens wanted to produce a sports-touring car using top-of-the-range Austin components, and the deal with Lord was that in return, Jensen would design and build a car for Austin in a similar vein. Eric Neale, who had joined Jensen as designer in 1946, submitted various designs, and the A40 sports-tourer was in essence a scaled-down Interceptor, although the production version was not as low-slung as Neale had intended, due to the need for higher ground clearance in certain export markets. Another vehicle for which Jensen tried out a body was the A90 Atlantic, and there was more of a family resemblance between contemporary Jensen and Austin models than the Americanized style which was sold from 1948 to 1952.

The Interceptor actually came out a year ahead of the Austin A40 Sports, thanks to a lot of hard graft and midnight oil burned in the factory. It was launched at the London Motor Show in 1949, its rounded graceful body the work of Jensen's Chief Engineer, Eric Neale, who employed a lengthened A70 chassis as a platform for the single carburettor version Sheerline engine. The Interceptor of 1950 could top 100mph (160kph), and 0–60mph (0–100kph) in just over 13 seconds. A fixed-head coupe was offered, the rear window of which prefigured the 541's styling, and the convertible was notable for the way in which the rigid Perspex rear and three-quarter windows sank into niches in the car's body when the hood was lowered.

Donald Healey showed off his new sports car at the 1952 Earls Court Show. The shape was styled by Healey's body designer and constructor, Gerry Coker, with Healey himself adding the distinctive original radiator-grille shape. There was extraordinary interest in it, with car fans queueing just for a glimpse. A deal had just been completed with Leonard Lord, which enabled Healey to

An early 1950s Jensen publicity shot for the Interceptor drophead Convertible.

Bearing similarities to the later MGA, Spitfire, and Sabre sports cars, this is a
development of the Eric Neale-designed Jensen prototype which should have
been seen at Earls Court in 1952, the very show where Donald Healey's sports
car took off. Austin's Leonard Lord was nevertheless sufficiently impressed by
this prototype to award Jensen the lucrative Healey contract.

With the rear glass hatch raised, there was very good access to the luggage
boot.

use the A90 2.6-litre straight-four engine and, as a very last-minute idea, the Tickford-built aluminium prototype was badged up as an Austin-Healey 100.

The original intention was that the car would be built by Tickfords at a rate of perhaps forty cars a week; Healey's own operation at Warwick was used to producing perhaps four cars a week. Jensen proposed to Lord that they could do rather better than that: how about 150 cars a week? To clinch the deal, Lord was shown a sports prototype of Neale's design, a car not unlike the forthcoming MGA in appearance, and Jensen were given the contract to build the Austin-Healey, which would support the company for fifteen years. Using rolling chassis made at Longbridge, Jensen produced all the completed painted and trimmed body-chassis units until the model's demise at the end of 1967. They built the first car within about six weeks of having the specification, and all were made by hand in aluminium. Donald Healey received a royalty for every car sold, but the Austin-Healey was rather more important to Jensen.

THE 541

By the time the Earls Court Motor Show came round in 1953, Jensen Motors were able to show their 541 grand-touring car, a fabulous-looking car, with rather more styling panache than the contemporary Aston Martin DB2/4. Designed by Eric Neale, with input from General Manager Colin Riekie, the show car was bodied in aluminium, although the production 541s were built of glassfibre. Alan Jensen was convinced that fibreglass was the material of the future for car bodies. At one motor show, he deliberately dropped something on the fibreglass to demonstrate that it would not dent. It was also a cheaper way to make bodies. With hindsight, of course, the problem which fibreglass usually encounters as

---

Pat Skidmore

Pat Skidmore started working at Jensen in 1963, and has worked mostly in the departments which handle the finishing of the cars. This involves installing all the interior trim, fitting the glass in doors and windscreens, the electric motors for window lifts, door handles, stereos, and all the fiddly little bits and pieces which we perhaps take for granted in our cars.

'When I joined, they were making about twenty Austin Healeys a day, and it was real hard work. They went up to 120 a week, with perhaps fifteen Interceptors as well.

'There's still a good market for this car. This is a problem for a lot of manufacturers today, because people don't want the ordinary run of the mill car. If they can afford it, they want something like an Interceptor. But none of us could afford one though. On a modern car, everything is robotized. At Jensen, the cars are made by hand, and it has always been like that. None of the parts have ever fitted. Even with the Austin Healey, one side was longer than the other. They took the Austin Healey away to Pressed Steel Fishers for about twelve months, and then it came back. Then they introduced the Interceptor in 1966. We'd get the finished car, including paint. It's cellulose even now; we don't do two-pack here, but some have been done to special order in two pack.'

'There's a good team spirit here, and we all pull together. If we have a problem we get Albert over to sort it out.'

---

time passes is surface crazing and, indeed, the beautiful wraparound rear window of the 541s is prone to crazing over and going opaque.

Stylistically, Jensens had always been pretty much 'state of the art', and the 541 was no exception. Its streamlined shape produced a Cd figure of 0.36, which is not at all bad even by today's standards. Mechanically, it relied on the tried and tested, continuing to use the 4-litre Austin unit, albeit with triple SU carburettors and

The first Interceptor was a well-appointed touring car, designed by Eric Neale, and first introduced in 1949. This is a 1953 model. It was based on an Austin A70 chassis and powered by the 4-litre Austin Sheerline engine.

special manifolds. The rest of the specification included cam and roller steering, wishbone and coil-spring front, semi-elliptic springs and live rear-axle suspension, derived from the A70 parts bin. The light fibreglass shell required a chassis of greater sophistication, however. Large-diameter tubes constituted the outriggers and a central box section provided strength.

The bodyshell was created in three sections, with aluminium door frames. Gaining access to the mechanicals was particularly easy, for the car had a huge one-piece bonnet and front wings. The 541's special trade mark was its swivelling air-intake for the radiator; it was operated by the driver, who could regulate the flow of cold air according to the ambient temper-

THE 541					
Mk no.	**Years**	**Engine series**	**Chassis no.**		
541	1953–58	DS4			541/
541R	1957–60	DS7			541R/
541R	1957–60	DS5			541R/
541S	1960–63	DS5	RHD	Auto	100/
			LHD	Manual	101/
			RHD	Manual	102/
			LHD	Auto (US)	103/

541 Series – Specification

Engine	DS5: Austin 6cyl, ohv 87 × 111mm, 3,993cc, 244cu in, 130bhp @ 3,700rpm, 3SU carbs. DS7: Austin 6cyl, ohv, 87 × 111mm, 3,993cc, 244cu in, 140bhp @ 3,700rpm, 2 SU carbs
Transmission	4 speed and overdrive, synchromesh on second, third and fourth.
Suspension	Front, independent: coil springs and wishbones. Rear, ½ elliptic springs.
Steering	541: Cam and roller. 541R and 2: Rack and pinion.
Structure	Box section and tubular steel chassis, glassfibre body.
Brakes	541: Hydraulic, 11in drums. 541 De Luxe, R and S: Hydraulic, servo, 11.25in discs all round.
Wheelbase	8ft 9in. Length 14ft 10in.

ature. Closing it produced an aerodynamic improvement of no less than 17 per cent.

The 541 De Luxe which came out in 1956 was the first production car to be offered with disc brakes all round, and this was something of a sensation at the time. Power output of the early 541 was rated at 125bhp, with a top speed of around 115mph (185kph). The engine produced so much torque that you could be doing 70mph (110kph) with the tachometer showing just over 2,000rpm. The better-geared 541R, which came out in 1957, used the Moss gearbox which Jaguar fitted at the time, coupled with the Laycock overdrive as standard; it was perhaps not as robust a unit as the regular wide-ratio Austin gearbox, however.

The 541R produced 140bhp, and specifications included either twin or triple SUs. The 'R' stood for rack-and-pinion steering, which conferred a more balanced feeling, and it was reckoned to be quite good in its day. Whereas the early 541s had drum brakes,

Competition appearances for Jensens have been rare, but here is a 541 driving through the tunnel under the circuit into the Brands Hatch paddock on 31 March 1957.

Surely Eric Neale's best design: the 1956 Jensen 541, fitted with wire wheels which tended to enhance the car's sporting appearance.

the 541R got powerful Dunlop disc brakes, with vacuum assistance coming from a reservoir housed in the nearside chassis tube. Many 541s were fitted with wire wheels, which, if anything, enhanced the car's sporting appearance. They were shod with cross-ply tyres in those days, of course, but matters are considerably improved if the car is equipped with radial tyres today. It came as a surprise to learn how few 541s were made, for Jensen built only 225 541 and 541 De Luxe models, and 193 541Rs.

When it was phased out in 1960, the 541R cost £2,707, including purchase tax, making it a cool £1,000 cheaper than an Aston Martin DB4, and £1,500 less than a Bristol

406. It was superseded by the 541S, similar in profile but substantially altered in its frontal aspect. Gone was the movable air-intake, which was replaced by conventional mesh grille and bonnet air scoop. Jensen were anxious to maintain the styling edge, and this new-look front brought the 541 back up to par with the trendy Italians. More fundamentally, the chassis rails were moved further apart and the suspension rearranged to provide wider track front and back.

The result was a wider interior space, with improved height and leg-room; even those banished to the rear seats were more fortunate. A four-speed Rolls-Royce 'hydra-matic' automatic transmission and limited-

The 541 in its final form was the 541S, which had a wider body than earlier models. Gone was the distinctive air flap over the radiator, in favour of a grille more in keeping with its 1961 contemporaries.

slip differential were optional, and the 541S was the first British production car with front seat-belts. Other creature comforts fitted as standard included a radio, fire extinguisher, spot lamps and first-aid kit.

SUBCONTRACT WORK

During the 541's early years, Jensen fortunes were most decidedly on the up, and it was in 1956 that production moved into the much larger factory premises at Kelvin Way, West Bromwich. Austin Healey production moved from Carters Green, along with the Tempo commercial vehicles. Other subcontract work soon came along. In 1959, Jensen Motors was given the go ahead to manufacture the bodies for Austin's answer to the Land-Rover, the Austin Gipsy. Austin had already been making a four-wheel-drive

off-road vehicle for the Army, the RR-engined Champ, but the Gipsy was intended to cream off some of the Land-Rover market. So secure was the Land-Rover's grasp of this segment that the Gipsy did not sell in sufficient numbers to make it a viable proposition; it was dropped in 1962.

In 1959, Jensen got the job of assembling, preparing and trimming the Volvo P1800 sports coupe, using bodyshells made at the new Pressed Steel plant at Linwood, near Glasgow. There was insufficient spare capacity at Volvo's own Gothenburg factory at the time, which is how Pressed Steel came to be involved. The concept was that some 150 painted bodies would be shipped to Sweden each week to be completed with all mechanicals installed by Volvo themselves. However, the scheme fell apart because of the generally poor standards of construction of the bodyshells at Linwood. Jensen found

Jensen Motors' West Bromwich premises at Carters Green were superseded by a new factory at Kelvin Way in 1956.

the arrangement uneconomical because so much making-good had to be done before their own share of the work could begin. Following inspections by Volvo representatives, it was not long before Volvo decided to produce the cars entirely in their own premises.

Jensen Motors' next adventure involved the Rootes Group and none other than Jack Brabham, World Champion in 1959 and 1966; the issue in question was how to increase the modest performance of the Sunbeam Alpine, a competent but unexciting sports car. Brabham suggested following the example of Texan racing-driver Carroll Shelby, who was making a success of shoe-horning Ford V8 engines into AC Aces and calling them Cobras, and Rootes were impressed. By 1963, a prototype was up and running, and Lord Rootes had done a deal with Henry Ford II. In looking around for a suitable base to manufacture what was to be the Sunbeam Tiger, Rootes contacted their one-time Design Engineer, Kevin Beattie, now Deputy Chief Engineer at Jensen. As a result, Jensen became heavily involved in the development of the car, as well as assembling and finishing it.

The Alpine was transformed, and the Tiger was a rumbling success for some five years. A round figure of 7,067 units were built, mostly for export, but things were not looking good financially for the Rootes Group. By 1967, they had been taken over by US giant Chrysler, who could not condone Ford engines in one of its own products and, in effect, that was the end of the Tiger.

With all this subcontract work going on, of which the Austin Healey was the most stable, production of 541s was only ever two or three cars a week, perhaps only one, and there were always buyers waiting for them. Back in 1959, the Jensen brothers had looked around for capital to expand further, and entered into an arrangement with the Norcros Group. Part of the deal was that Michael Day would become Managing Director, since the Jensen brothers, who alternated as Chairman on a year-by-year basis, were fast approaching retirement age. The division of the company started at this point.

C-V8 Series – Specification	
Engine	Mk I and II: Chrysler V8, ohv, 105 × 86mm, 5,916cc, 361cu in, 305bhp @ 4,800rpm, Carter carb. Mk II and III: Chrysler V8, ohv, 108 × 86mm, 6,276cc, 383cu in, 330bhp @ 4,600rpm, Carter carb.
Transmission	Chrysler Torqueflite 3-speed automatic. Powerlock differential, 4-speed manual option.
Suspension	Front, independent coil springs and wishbones. Rear, ½ elliptic springs.
Steering	Rack and pinion.
Structure	Box section and tubular steel chassis, glassfibre body.
Brakes	Hydraulic, servo, 11.25in discs all round. Mk III dual circuits.
Wheelbase	8ft 9in. Length 15ft 4.5in.

The most controversial styling feature of the C-V8 was the twin slant headlights. Eric Neale's original plan was to clad the lights in a Perspex cowl, but it was found to impair illumination and a chrome surround was fitted as a substitute.

THE C-V8

The early sixties was a very different period from the previous one. Gone was the austerity, replaced with a rampant flowering of new ideas, designs and use of colour, and there was a new Jensen for the new decade. With the 541S's successor, the C-V8, we are getting into the concept of the modern Interceptor. For although the C-V8 continues the same stylistic ideas inherent in the 541, perhaps producing a more re-strained overall effect, slant-eyed headlights not withstanding, its performance and character are transformed by the adoption of the 305bhp 5.9-litre 'Golden Commando' Chrysler V8.

THE C-V8					
Mk no.	**Years**	**Engine series**	**Chassis no.**		
Mk I	1962–63	S	RHD	Auto	104/
		S	LHD	Auto	106/
Mk II	1963–65	S	LHD	Auto	106/
		S	RHD	Manual	105/
		S	RHD	Auto	107/
		V	RHD	Auto	108/
		V	LHD	Auto	110/
Mk III	1965–66	V	RHD	Auto	111/
		A	RHD	Auto	112/
		A	LHD	Auto	113/
		A	RHD	Manual	114/

Exit one V8, on its way to being stripped down and rebuilt.

The fibreglass-bodied 1965 Mark III C-V8 was a genuine four seater, powered by the 6,276cc Chrysler V8, which produced 330bhp. A new feature was dual-circuit brakes.

This understressed lazy lump drives through the well-proven Torqueflite automatic gearbox, giving a top speed of 132mph (212.4kph) and a 0–60mph (0–100kph) time of 8.2 seconds. The controversial double-headlight treatment was originally intended by designer Eric Neale to be clad in Perspex cowls, but the idea was abandoned because of the detrimental effect it had on the headlamp beam. As for the look of it, nobody casts aspersions at the contemporary Ferrari 300.

First shown at Earls Court in 1962, the C-V8 found Jensen to be yet again the innovators, for it was first to be fitted with an alternator instead of a dynamo. The C-V8 placed Jensen firmly in the luxury-touring-car segment; many little details were thoughtfully included in the car, such as the leather pull inside the door pockets, which enabled the inside of this small edifice to be cleaned out. The next significant improvement was the fitment of Armstrong Selectaride adjustable dampers, closely followed by the replacement of the 5.9-litre unit by Chrysler's 6.3-litre offering, and the model became the Mark II. This brought power up to 330bhp and a 140mph (225kph) potential. Three years later the company made a quantum leap when it produced the C-V8 FF with Ferguson four-wheel drive and Dunlop Maxaret anti-lock brakes.

The next move take us into the realms of our subject, the Interceptor.

2 The Interceptor

POLITICAL EXPEDIENTS

Although the Interceptor was in series production for some ten years from 1966 to 1976, setting aside for a moment its renaissance in 1983, it was the inception of this model which brought about the most fundamental changes in the company. It was the cause of the Jensen brothers' departure, despite the fact that they were either near to or in the throes of retirement anyway. And without their presence in the company, as notional figureheads at any rate, in the longer term there was not the goodwill or influence which they probably would have commanded to find the capital to shore up the ailing company before the crash came.

Jensen Motors was in a sense also a political victim, since the board was unable to persuade the Labour government of 1975 to rescue the company. Jensen was not alone; it was a time of world crisis in the motor industry, with firms as diverse as Rolls Royce and Mazda in difficulties, and British Leyland was brought into public ownership in 1975. So perhaps 700 jobs in the West Midlands didn't amount to much. The same Labour government had just helped out Chrysler to the tune of £162 million in 1975, to enable the restructuring of the company's UK operation and the Linwood plant in particular. Cynics might point out that Linwood is close to Paisley, traditionally strong Labour territory, and some 8,400 jobs were on the line there.

There are two further ironies in this episode. The first is that despite the shoring-up operation, Linwood was closed down in 1979 in a deal with Peugeot-Citröen, and the second is that the DeLorean plant in Belfast was funded to the hilt, ratified by the Tory regime in an effort to appease the political hornets' nest in Northern Ireland. Perhaps the answer to this is that Linwood and Belfast qualified for regional aid, whereas the West Midlands did not. It could also be argued that a luxury-car manufacturer such as Jensen was unlikely to qualify for state aid under a Labour government.

Whatever you make of this, one thing is certain. Jensen was a company with integrity, and it went down for the sake of a couple of million pounds, whilst less than a decade later, something like fifty times that figure went into the DeLorean operation, which produced only a handful of vehicles that were conceptually flawed from the outset. You can take this comparison as far as you like, for just as an absence of the Jensen brothers at the helm may have contributed to the failure of Jensen Motors, the DeLorean affair undoubtedly hastened the end of Colin Chapman, so that things would never be the same again at Lotus.

CONCEPTION OF THE INTERCEPTOR

The Jensen brothers had always had a hand in designing their own cars, but treated it more as a hobby, turning out a couple of cars a week, maybe only one, perhaps none in a bad week. This was true of the big pre-war models, the early 1950s aluminium-bodied Interceptor, the 541 and the C-V8. The company made its money from subcontract work, essentially from Austin. Jensen's own cars were the icing on the cake, which attracted the attention of the rest of the

Mark I Interceptors nearing completion at the factory in 1968.

motor industry and, ostensibly, they built more or less what they wanted. In general, Jensen cars cost more to build than they could be sold for, and this was to include the Mark I Interceptors. In the late 1950s, the brothers went to Norcros, a holding company, with a view to expanding and placing Jensen Motors in a stronger position when tendering for contract work. In 1957, Jensen became part of the Norcros Group.

Then they took on a young man who had been with the Rootes Group's Chrysler subsidiary in Australia for a couple of years. Kevin Beattie was a brilliant engineer; aged thirty-three at the time, he joined Jensen in 1960 as Deputy Chief Engineer. He was responsible for designing, some people say over-designing, the chassis for the C-V8, which was clad in a body penned by Company Designer Eric Neale, although it was said Beattie never liked the C-V8's styling.

THE P66

By 1964, Eric Neale and Richard Jensen were laying out the plans for Jensen's own replacement for the Austin Healey, code-named the P66, which was intended to be a much cheaper car than the C-V8. Richard Jensen was pondering how to use the spare capacity within the plant should the Healey contract with BMC elapse. He felt, probably quite rightly, that the US market would continue to buy traditional open-top European sports cars of the Austin Healey variety, despite the conviction in the UK that the sports car was in decline, and that people were tired of wind-in-the-hair motoring. The Healey, and to a lesser extent the Tiger because of its lower volume, were great dollar earners for Jensen, and Richard had the vision to appreciate what would happen when there were no more Healeys to sell. He got wind of the fact that Donald Healey was not exactly popular with BMC Chairman George Harriman, who was of the opinion that Healey was doing rather too well out of his car.

Accordingly, Eric Neale drew up plans for what Jensen hoped would use up the spare capacity if the Healey stopped being made. The P66, which was also intended to be known as the Interceptor, would have a new outrigger-tubed chassis, more akin to the 541

Kevin Beattie

Born in South Africa in 1927, Kevin Beattie was educated in the UK. After his father's death he went to work for the Rootes Group whose training scheme enabled him to read for an engineering degree at the University of London. Beattie gained a thorough knowledge of automobile engineering at Rootes, and was set for a distinguished career with Chrysler, their Australian subsidiary. However, he contracted a serious liver infection *en route* to Australia, which kept him out of action for some time.

Beattie's career progressed with Rootes in Australia, with serious offers tempting him to move to both Holden and BMC there, but the Australian environment did not altogether agree with his wife Eileen, and Beattie moved the family back to the UK, and himself to Rootes's British operation.

Beattie was employed Deputy Chief Engineer at Jensen Motors on 1 January 1960, and his first major project was to design the chassis for the new C-V8 model. However, he was less than happy with Eric Neale's design of the C-V8's glassfibre bodyshell, and went off to Italy to see what the fashionable Italian styling houses could offer. He returned from Turin and Milan with drawings based on the C-V8 chassis from Touring of Milan, Alfredo Vignale and Ghia, he was able to persuade the Norcros half of the Jensen board that the Italian body was the one to go with, rather than an in-house job.

The design most favoured was originally penned by Touring's studio, but Beattie had it altered by Vignale's draughtsman. When the board voted to go for the new Interceptor design, Vignale got the job of producing the prototype because of Touring's lack of capacity and ailing financial situation. Although the specialist *carrozzerie* of the Italian motor industry produce fabulous cars in aluminium, there is no tradition of working in fibreglass, so the Interceptor would be in steel.

With the introduction of the Interceptor, the rift at Jensen was complete. Designer Eric Neale resigned almost immediately, as did the elderly Jensen brothers, and forever afterwards they blamed Kevin Beattie for causing the schism. He, however, visualized the Interceptor as being the right car for Jensen to be producing, a view shared by Carl Duerr when he was hired in 1967; the problem at that stage was that the Interceptor was unviable without the support of a major subcontract project like the Austin Healey had been.

With the acquisition of Jensen Motors by Wm. Brandt's bank, Beattie became a board member, but his special engineering talent was hard at work refining and developing the Interceptor and FF models, and searching for a successor to the Austin Healey. When Kjell Qvale took over in 1970, Beattie was pressed into action to develop Donald Healey's idea for the Jensen Healey prototype.

A design by William Towns was eventually selected, and Beattie was controller of the operation,

The man largely responsible for the introduction of the Interceptor, Kevin Beattie worked for Jensen Motors from 1960 until he died, in 1975.

The Jensen-Healey GT, which was stylistically an excellent solution to the problem of putting a top on the sports car and giving it a capacious luggage boot. However, the company went into liquidation when only 473 GTs had been built.

with body and chassis development under the guiding hand of Jensen's own Brian Spicer. A major source of components was to be the Vauxhall parts bin, and engines would come, without guarantee or any meaningful development, from Lotus. Qvale required 200 Jensen Healeys to be built each week, more or less from the word go, and the production team managed to progress from prototype to production line in less than two years.

Simultaneously, Beattie was also working with Spicer on the development of the F-Type, intended, as the Esperado, to be the sucessor to the Interceptor. Designs were commissioned from Italy again, but a Towns style was once again chosen. An enlarged Interceptor chassis was the basis for testing, and the bodywork featured bulbous racing-style wheelarches to accommodate the wider track and fatter tyres. Somewhat predictably, this prototype hack was known as Big Bertha.

The Mark II Jensen Healey came out in mid-1973, and Beattie was now Managing Director; the Mk III Jensen Healey appeared just over a year later, and had a five-speed gearbox. The final incarnation of the Jensen Healey was the GT, mechanically similar in specification but more luxuriously appointed and, being a sports estate, aimed at a different segment to the sports car. With Donald Healey having left the board in 1974, the car was simply known as the Jensen GT. Only 473 were ever built. The two final variations on the Interceptor theme were in the pipeline in 1974: the Convertible and the Coupe.

It was in this hectic environment that Beattie's health took another dive and, in October 1974, he was forced to stand down. A year later, aged only forty-eight, he was dead.

than the C-V8, with steel inner sections and aluminium panels. It was to be powered by the familiar 6.3-litre Chrysler unit, with 4.5-litre and 5.9-litre V8s as options.

The first prototype was launched at the Earls Court show in 1965 to much acclaim, for it was a very sleek-looking car with contemporary Italianate lines not unlike those of a Maserati Mistrale or Sebring perhaps, and with its lazy American V8, it was capable of 140mph (225kph).

The P66 was rushed into prototype when it was clear that BMC would axe the Healey 3000, ostensibly in the face of US safety regulations. There was some surprise that the car was a soft-top, and over a thousand pounds cheaper than the C-V8: it was not fully grasped that the P66 was a replacement for the Healey rather than the C-V8. A second prototype was built with a hard top, and the order book looked promising.

However, Neale and Jensen were forestalled by the Norcros management who, under Beattie's guidance, decided that in fact what was wanted was a C-V8 replacement. In any case, Beattie had decided that

the P66 looked too traditional. The fashion in 1965 or thereabouts, which must have been complete anathema to the Jensen brothers, was to get the Italians to design your car for you. Aston Martin had been to Touring of Milan, Alvis had gone to Graber of Switzerland, Triumph went to Michelotti, and Pinin Farina was busy with virtually the whole of the BMC range. On the whole, the Italian styling houses create fabulous-looking cars.

Whilst Kevin Beattie was courting the Italian *carrozzerie* in search of a new design to supersede the C-V8, the Jensen board was divided, and this at a time when Richard Jensen had just had a heart attack and was convalescing in hospital. Norcros management, including Principal John Boex and Managing Director Brian Owen, along with Kevin Beattie, were in favour of a direct replacement for the C-V8, preferably styled by a fashionable Italian design house, for it was felt, by Beattie in particular, that the C-V8 concept badly needed updating. It was, after all, not that dissimilar to the overall appearance of the 541S. So when Kevin

The second P66 prototype was intended to replace the factory capacity vacated by the Austin Healey rather than succeed the C-V8.

The second of the P66 prototypes, photographed in the US, where it suffers from a poorly-located American number-plate. The UK registration is correct but the plate should be white on black. Unlike the first prototype which was a Convertible, this car was designed as a Coupe because it was felt that the world sports car market was turning away from the Convertible.

Second of the P66 prototypes, photographed at the Jensen factory on 5 April 1966. This view shows the modified rear lamps and spare-wheel access.

Beattie returned from Turin and Milan with drawings based on the C-V8 chassis from *carrozzerie* Touring Superleggera, Alfredo Vignale and Ghia, the writing was on the wall.

The scheme most liked was the one from Touring's studio, but Beattie had it altered by Vignale's draughtsman. Back at West Bromwich, Eric Neale put the final touches to what was to become the Mark I Interceptor. Because Vignale had adapted the 'Superleggera' Touring design and, on account of Touring's precipitous financial position in 1966, its lack of capacity and imminent absorption into Alfa Romeo, Vignale was commissioned to build the prototype.

There was a considerable amount of bad feeling in the Jensen factory at this point, for it was abundantly clear that the P66 was being ignored by the powerful Norcros end of the board; out-manoeuvred and out-voted, a despondent Eric Neale tendered his resignation, feeling that his contribution to the

---

Vignale

The reputation of Alfredo Vignale's car body-building business was founded on the strength and rigidity of his products. The Italian racing driver Luigi Villoresi once somersaulted a Vignale-bodied Ferrari going at over 100mph (160kph), and his survival with just cuts and bruises was said to have been due to the solidity of his car.

Alfredo Vignale set up his workshop in Turin with his brothers Giovanni and Giuseppe in 1946, and the firm's reputation quickly developed as a result of a special body made for a Fiat Topolino. It was admired by Lancia, who commissioned the Vignale brothers to create a design for the new Aprilia.

The Vignale *carrozzeria* worked in both steel and aluminium with such confidence and dexterity that very often they dispensed with the customary clay model and went straight to the wooden maquette, and the car took shape as the anvil-beaten metal panels were placed over it. It took a great deal of skill to judge the curves with the naked eye.

After the Lancia commission, Vignale was suddenly in demand, and both Alfa Romeo and Maserati ordered racy bodies for their sports models; Vignale produced the 230bhp Alfa Romeo Sport Speciale and the Maserati 6AG of 1951. They were quickly followed by the Ferrari 212 and 340 America Coupes, but Vignale was quite capable of turning its hand to more utilitarian vehicles like the Lancia Aprilia Berlina. Commissions from Fiat came in the shape of the 1100 Cabriolet, which had a grille reminiscent of an Alfa, and spats over the back wheels. This theme was taken further in a Vignale-styled Fiat 1500 Coupe, which had spats over the front wheels as well.

Vignale produced one-off prototype bodies for Rolls Royce and Fiat, and marketed cars under its own name, built on Fiat 600D and 1300 chassis. At the time Kevin Beattie was in Turin shopping for a stylist for the Interceptor, Vignale's best-known work was probably the Maserati 3500 sports car, built between 1960 and 1962; some 240 units were made. Beattie handed Vignale the original designs for the Interceptor which had been done in the Touring studios, and Vignale adapted them. The arrangement between Jensen Motors and Vignale was that Vignale would build the cars and market them in Europe through its associate company Sincar, headed by Carlo Dusio. However, it was not to be a lasting situation, because the cars were not built to the standards expected by Jensen, and Sincar was able to undercut the UK price in mainland Europe by not having to pay import tariffs.

By 1967, the deal was off, and after only fifty cars had been made, all the jigs and machine tools were brought over to West Bromwich, where Interceptor production took off again. In 1969, the Vignale factory at Grugliasco was acquired by Carrozzeria Ghia, itself destined soon to become a satellite of the Ford Motor Company, and three days after the takeover, Alfredo Vignale was killed in an accident in his Maserati.

Vignale carried on building cars for Ghia, including the de Tomaso Pantera, until 1975.

The very first Interceptor. This is the Vignale prototype, built in Italy on a
C-V8 chassis, engine and drive-train. It was first registered in the UK in
September 1966.

The Interceptor prototype does not have a regular Jensen chassis number;
instead it has chassis number EXP 115, marking it out as an experimental
vehicle.

Interceptor project was minimal, for he had scarcely been involved at all with it. Within weeks, the ailing Jensen brothers too decided to resign, feeling let down and snubbed by the rest of the board. Richard went to live in Malta for some years, where he died, and Alan lives a reclusive existence in Eastbourne. The final straw as far as Richard Jensen was concerned, was that his leaving present, which was a C-V8 straight off the production line, was painted blue, when it was well known that all his cars were of a pale bronze hue. The mistake was rectified, but it was a shabby end to a career of innovative genius and enthusiasm.

It was said that when the Jensen brothers found out about the Interceptor, the P66 convertible was cut up in a fit of pique. The amount of bad feeling borne by the Jensens can be gauged by Richard Jensen's reaction to a print he was given of a painting, commissioned to commemorate the company's Golden Jubilee in 1984. The painting hangs in the boardroom today, and it depicts all the people and cars which have ever been associated with the company. When he was commissioned, the artist was told to feature Kevin Beattie prominently, not so much as an epitaph to Beattie, who gave so much of himself to the company, but because in many ways he represented a fulcrum around which many of Jensen's central historical issues revolved. Richard Jensen returned his copy of the painting, declaring that he hardly recognized himself or his brother, and why was Kevin Beattie in prime position? As far as Richard Jensen was concerned, Beattie was always the villain of the piece. The Interceptor was Beattie's baby, and neither of the Jensens forgot that.

THE VIGNALE PROTOTYPE

In the spring of 1966, a C-V8 (chassis number 104/2142) was dispatched to the Vignale *carrozzeria*, where its fibreglass body was unbolted, and replaced with the all-steel Interceptor panels. Nowadays you'd have the scoop photographers of the motoring press like Hans Lehmann lurking around for a first glimpse of the prototype but, as it was, Kevin Beattie seemed to have got away with his four-day test run through the Alpine foothills of northern Italy without being spotted. Six months later, the first consignment of the Vignale bodies arrived at West Bromwich, and the Interceptor, along with its FF sibling, was ready for the Earls Court Show in mid-October.

At the time, the Jensen marque was still not widely known, and thought by many, on account of the Scandinavian-sounding name, to be a foreign manufacturer. The Interceptor's predecessors had been stylistically on the ball, and so it was with the Interceptor. The aspect which astonished most people at the time was the sheer size of the rear window. Some of us who fancied the look of the contemporary TVRs of the early 1960s, which had a similar arrangement in perspex, were amazed at the audacity of creating such a large space in glass. Others were to go some way to copying it, like AMC's Javelin, but it remains the Interceptor Saloon's outstanding visual hallmark. It was a car very much at the other end of the market for my contemporaries and myself, obsessed with motor racing and bent on emulating on-track spectacles in our day-to-day motoring.

The last Healey was shipped in December 1967. Suddenly the Jensen factory was virtually empty, and within a matter of months Norcros and the Jensen board were in deep financial trouble. Turnover fell from £200,000–300,000 a month to around £100,000, and profits crashed from £183,000 in 1966 to a loss of £82,000 in 1967; for four months running, losses had exceeded £25,000, and 800 men out of the 1,400 workforce were laid off. The nature of the Interceptor was such that the slightest hold-up in supply of components stalled production, and so cash flow fluctuated wildly.

The Interceptor was a complex sophisticated luxury vehicle compared with the Healey; completely different levels of production costs, labour input and marketing problems were involved, and Norcros and the Jensen management were in a quandary: should they cut production and start all over again, or should they continue and allow the backlog of half-finished cars to accumulate? Norcros Managing Director John Boex commissioned a firm of management consultants to recommend what to do, and they came up with a company 'doctor' called Carl Duerr, who agreed to act as Managing Director and try and sort things out.

DESPERATE REMEDIES

The atmosphere which greeted Duerr was one of gloom and despondency, for even the Norcros Chairman had gone on record, probably unsuspectingly, as saying that Jensen Motors was 'not a suitable investment'. No one at Jensen really knew where they stood in respect of leadership, the figurehead of the Jensens themselves now removed, and the situation was compounded by recent productivity agreements which allowed each person more free time. To make matters worse, there were still engineering details to be sorted out on the Interceptors, and quality control ensured that there were some thirty cars lying unsold because of deficiencies of one sort or another. This

During the period of Carl Duerr's Managing Directorship, Jensen Motors relied heavily on the combined Public Relations skills of Tony Good (left), Gethin Bradley and Richard Graves (right), to lift the sales and marketing pitch of the Interceptor. Carl Duerr (second from right) listens to Tony Good's plan for promoting the Mark II.

Now the property of Christchurch enthusiast Bryn Shaw, the prototype Interceptor has had three owners from 1969, when it was sold by the factory.

The prototype never had power-assisted steering, and it was probably unique in this. The automatic shift did not have a 'park' position.

The prototype displays Mark I bumpers with pointed overriders, body-coloured setting for headlamps, relatively narrow tyres with white-wall detailing, on Rostyle wheels.

Detailing of the prototype's waistline, with Mark I rear-light cluster and pointed overrider. Exhaust pipes are neatly let in to the rear valance.

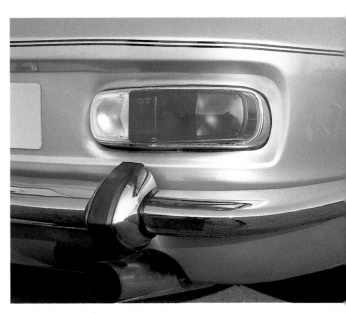

Carl Duerr

Carl Duerr was born in Chicago in 1916 and, after gaining an engineering degree, he had a varied career as a management consultant, working in over twenty countries. At the end of the Second World War, he was appointed Allied Chief of Industry in Austria with a view to setting up the Austrian economy in the wake of hostilities.

In 1967, when Austin Healey production was being closed down at Jensen and the company looked a decidedly unappealing prospect, even to its owners the Norcros Group, a firm of management consultants, Booz, Allen and Hamilton, was appointed to advise on what should be done for the best. They in turn nominated Carl Duerr, whose profession by now was 'Company Doctor', based at his Inter-Counsel Establishment at the tiny independent kingdom of Liechtenstein. Duerr had never even heard of Jensen cars at the time, and the sales catalogues he had access to depicted the C-V8, by then somewhat dated, and could hardly be said to have filled him with enthusiasm. Nevertheless, he agreed to act as Jensen Motors' Managing Director in place of Brian Owen, with a view to turning the company around and preparing it for sale to a suitable bidder.

Life was far from easy for Duerr, for he was faced with commuting at weekends to and from Munich, to be with his wife Marianna. However, it was his German connections which led him to view the Interceptor as a promising export commodity, because it seemed to him that the German motor manufacturers had no comparable vehicle. Duerr would always drive himself around in Interceptors, as much as a quality control exercise as a means of transport, and he grew to appreciate the Interceptor's qualities as a vehicle ideal for senior management personnel who wanted to drive themselves rather than be chauffeured around. There was much potential, he thought, in getting cars sold in Germany.

He finally severed the Vignale connection by buying out the sales operation called Sincar, headed by Carlo Dusio, which had been marketing the inferior Vignale-built Interceptors at import tax-free EEC prices in Europe. The next step was to ensure that West Bromwich-built cars were sufficiently well-made for the particular German market.

Duerr's expertise also lay in management consultancy, based on years spent in similar exercises as the Jensen turnaround. He had reorganized Europe's largest retail jewellery-store chain, raised the production and sales of a German woollen mill by 600 per cent, and placed an industrial equipment manufacturer in profit for the first time after eight years of trading. He had set up refineries throughout Europe, Africa and the Middle East for a vegetable oil producer, and prior to going to Jensen Motors Limited, he was a non-executive Director on the main board of J. Bibby and Sons, the UK food conglomerate. After leaving Jensen in 1970, he supervised the recovery of Bibby's Italian operation of which he was President, from a loss-maker in 1970, to profit-maker in 1971.

His thoughts, observations and reminiscences are recorded in light-hearted style in his book on corporate communication, entitled *Management Kinetics*, written shortly after his departure from Jensen. Aside from the need to improve the product, Duerr identified three areas in which Jensen Motors needed to be improved: the first was the poor standard of management-employee relations, which led to low morale; the second was the question of ownership, which had been the absentee Norcros group after the departure of the Jensen brothers; and the third factor was subcontract work, which had kept the company buoyant for so long, but by 1968 was non-existent.

By June 1968, after less than eighteen months at Jensen, Duerr had masterminded the sale of Jensen from Norcros to the merchant bankers Wm. Brandt's Sons and Company Ltd, in a deal which gave him and his co-directors a 38 per cent stake in the company. From a practical point of view, Duerr had raised output from perhaps two or three cars a week in 1967 to ten or twelve in 1969, and August 1969 saw the production of the thousandth Interceptor.

However, with the credit squeeze of 1970, the banks were becoming nervous, and insisted on a curtailment of Duerr's expansion programme. The work he had been taken on to do was complete when he introduced Kjell Qvale to Brandt's in the spring of 1970. Carl Duerr remained his active, dynamic and personable self until he died in 1987.

represented perhaps £150,000 worth of stock, and it degenerated by the day as cars were cannibalized for parts to finish other vehicles. Morale was so low that one section blamed another when parts did not fit, and this became a vicious circle of passing the buck.

The years 1967–70 may have been difficult times for Jensen – indeed, things were never so desperate as late 1967 to early 1968, but they were probably the most fruitful in terms of morale and rationalization. This was entirely due to the presence of Carl Duerr, by all accounts a 'terrific guy', and a man with a 'magnetic personality'. Duerr was brought in by Norcros from his Liechtenstein 'surgery', Inter-Counsel Establishment, to get Jensen Motors into shape and prepare the company for sale. He had worked virtually all over the world, and had done his time as a washer-up on the SS Atlantic Empire and on the shop-floor at Capstan Machine Co, Cleveland, in the early days of unionization. In his prime, Duerr was pretty adventurous, on both sides of the Atlantic.

He always drove the Interceptor himself, as a kind of quality-control monitor, but he soon became convinced of its sales potential; it was the car itself which endeared him to the Jensen cause in the first place. He saw an export niche for the car in Europe, particularly in Germany, where it filled a gap above the Mercedes SL and 500SLK, which were, if anything, rather smaller inside, and without the brute power of the Jensen. Porsche were a decade away from introducing their closest equivalent, the 928, and the six- and seven-Series BMWs were also a long way off. The Germans simply didn't have a car which Duerr believed appropriate for the use of the managing director, chairman or president of a company, who might want to drive himself to work.

When asked in an interview in the *Evening Standard* in 1968 whether it really needed an American to sort out Jensen's affairs, Duerr replied tartly, 'Yes, it does, because it's in a mess. But give me a year or so and I'll get it into shape so that a gentleman can run it.'

It was early days for the Interceptor, of course, and most people were still unfamiliar with the car. With an eye to the public relations function, Duerr contrived with his PR associates, Tony Good and Gethin Bradley of Good Relations/Assets in Action, to get Interceptors into various films, such as the series *The Protectors*, in which Robert Vaughan drove a Mark II. He sold cars to people considered fashionable by potential Jensen owners: stars like Tony Jacklin, Frank Sinatra and Cliff Richard. There were frequent press conferences and interviews on television and in the media. But this was when the company was starting to swing back up. First, there were serious problems to be overcome, not least of which was to get the product right and, more fundamentally, Duerr perceived three areas which contributed to the malaise at Jensen, which had to be attended to.

THE TROUBLE WITH JENSEN

The first factor was labour relations, the second was problems with subcontract work, and the third, uncertainty as to who would eventually own the company. All of this was undermining morale. And, basically, Duerr knew the Interceptor was just too cheap. He diagnosed a void between the shop-floor and management, and determined to close it to improve morale and productivity. One of his first moves was to institute the same 8.00 a.m. clocking-in times for both 'white' and 'blue collar' workers. In order to streamline the operation, 150 workers out of 500 were given their cards, and shop stewards were told that Duerr's goal was 50 per cent more cars with 25 per cent fewer people. This was tricky, for there were no less than sixteen unions represented within the company –

The Rich and Famous

The Interceptor was the kind of car owned by sportsmen and celebrities who had 'made it' to the top of their profession, like Frank Sinatra, golf stars Jack Nicklaus and Tony Jacklin (who wrote off his car), and rock stars Ginger Baker and John Bonham (the late Led Zeppelin drummer). Keith Richard of the Stones has just ordered one. Pop singer Lulu had one; slightly earlier, Susan Maughan had a black C-V8, with black interior, and, if memory serves, she had black hair and was always dressed in black. Actress Rita Tushingham had an FF, which was a big car for a relatively small woman. Cliff Richard had a Mark I Interceptor built for him; disc Jockey David Jacobs owned another. Film stars like Tony Curtis were Interceptor material, and novelist Harold Robbins had two or three cars of the Jensen marque.

More recently, the Interceptor has made a comeback on the screen as the car for a series called *The Baron*, and features large in the new *Saint* series with Simon Dutton as Simon Templar. I heard this vehicle described in the works as a 'rubbish car' though. I suppose it is fitting that hero Simon Templar progresses from Volvo P1800 to Interceptor, since both cars emanated from West Bromwich, for a while in the case of the Volvo at least. There was a period when the Templar character drove an XJ-S, but that must have been regarded as too flashy or high-profile. I watched a video which contained rushes of Gregory Peck sawing away at the wheel of an Interceptor Convertible in a most unnecessary fashion during the filming of *The Omen*; the stunt driving was all done at the Ministry of Defence's Chobham test track.

Comedy duos also seem to have had a penchant for the rumbling grand tourer: Morecambe and Wise had one each, and it was said that Ernie Wise was a difficult customer who used to spend a lot of time at the factory, although they hardly saw Eric Morecambe. Mike and Bernie Winters were another pair, of whom Mike was a difficult man to satisfy, unlike his partner.

The Jensen Interceptor market at the moment is the province of the very wealthy. The cars in build are virtually all Convertibles, and there appeared to have been a misunderstanding recently when the Prince of Morocco ordered a blue one with white trim, and when it came time for him to take delivery, he said he didn't want '. . . one like that, I want one with the big windscreen in the back.' So they started again, and within a week had transformed the car from Convertible to Saloon. It turned out he wanted it to be exactly the same as his father's, because his father won't let anyone else drive his car. It had to be identical, right down to the colour and number-plates.

A customized Interceptor wearing New York plates. Do the side skirts, wheel-arch spats and Corvette-style rear lights do the Interceptor any favours?

about twenty people to one union. The new clocking-in time so incensed the secretaries that they promptly unionized themselves, thus creating yet another union. The largest was the National Union of Vehicle Builders and the smallest and most significant the Midland Sheet Metalworkers' Society. Duerr eventually managed to get both unions together to thrash out his proposals for rationalizing the workforce.

Duerr is on record as saying that the workforce was 'bloody-minded'. 'But,' he said, 'if you point them in the right way, they'll get the job done. Bloody-mindedness becomes steadfastness, which is a necessary quality for building luxury cars.' He saw the Jensen workforce as 'inheriting the centuries-old tradition of metalworking craftsmanship', which endowed them with a high degree of technical integrity. This, thought Duerr, made for a workforce which took pride in its work, given the right motivation. Duerr was an expert in the deployment of persuasive tact, both on the shop-floor and in the boardroom, where the atmosphere was one of mutual respect. Duerr seems to have been readily accepted by the Jensen personnel because he was so obviously a foreigner.

One ploy during the redundancies period was to sack some of the inspectors in order to place the onus for quality control back on the men who were actually building the cars, and to a great extent they seemed to respond well to this. Later on some of the inspectors were re-employed. Duerr's management expertise was balanced against the motor industry experience of Richard Graves, Marketing Director; Kevin Beattie, Engineering Director; Tony Good, the company's Public Relations man who Duerr had elected to the board; and Bill Silvester, Production Manager. It was then a matter of getting everything to gel. As the cars improved, so did the enthusiasm of the workforce, and Duerr set down a four-point creed for the employees:

1. You have to go home tired in the evening.
2. You must make good money.
3. You have to enjoy your day's work.
4. You should be proud of it.

One of his moves to create a more cohesive atmosphere within the company was to instigate factory tours once a month for all the office staff to familiarize them with the production process. The guided tour was extended to include the families and friends of the workforce, and Duerr himself would as often as not act as the guide. It was the case that the wives of some of the men who had been at Jensen for perhaps twenty years had not the slightest idea of what they did. Within eighteen months there was sufficient confidence for card-carrying union members to staff the Jensen stand at the Earls Court Show, and free trips were run from the factory to the Show for employees, past and present. Their friends and families could come along for a £1 a person.

When Duerr arrived at West Bromwich at the end of 1967, the factory was producing just three cars a week, together with a great deal of BMC subcontract work. In eighteen months, production of Interceptors had risen to three cars a day, and subcontract work had ceased altogether. Duerr insisted on consolidating the home market before launching an export drive, with a priority for service and spares, but his aim was to supply twenty cars for the UK market, twenty for Europe, building up to forty for the US market within two years. It never got there, as we know, but there was at least something to motivate the company.

ENTER THE MERCHANT BANKERS

By July 1968 a scheme had been devised for devolving Jensen from Norcros. Merchant Bankers Wm. Brandt's Sons and Co. entered

THE INTERCEPTOR

Mk no.	Years	Engine series	Chassis no.		
Mk I	1966–69		RHD	Auto	115/
			RHD	Manual	116/
			LHD	Auto	117/
			RHD	Manual	118/
FF I	1966–69		RHD		119/
			LHD		120/
Mk II	1969–71		RHD		123/
			LHD		125/
			LHD	US Spec	125N/
FF II	1969–71		RHD		127/
Mk III	1971–73	G and H	RHD		128/
		G and H	LHD	Europe	129/
		G and H	LHD	US Spec	133/
	1973–76	J	RHD		136/
		J	LHD	Europe	137/
		J	LHD	US Spec	140/
FF III	1971	E	RHD		130/
SP	1971–73	G and H	RHD		131/
		G and H	LHD	Europe	132/
		H	LHD	US Spec	134/
		H	RHD		138/
Convertible (incl. Mk IV)	1974–76 (1974–90)		1974 onwards		
Coupe	1975–76		*See* under specification		

the picture at this point, becoming major shareholders, with the balance of the shares going to the board members. The advantage of Jensen belonging to a Merchant Bank was that it would be able to absorb cash-flow fluctuations and free the management to concentrate on running the company.

Jensen Motors seemed to be just about breaking even by now, with production running at around fifteen cars a week. There was £1m in the bank, which was the result of a bid to pacify prospective owners who had yet to take delivery of their cars. Duerr made it known that Jensen intended to put the prices of the cars up, and customers were given the incentive of paying for their car in full before the 1 July deadline when prices were set to rise – the Interceptor to £5,200 and the FF to £7,000, regardless of whether their car was ready for delivery or not. Many customers and dealers responded, and the interest earned Jensen the £1m, which made

the picture look less bleak as far as Wm. Brandt's Sons and Co. were concerned.

In fact, prospects looked good for going public in 1972, when it was envisaged that Jensen Motors would be capable of relying on its own products to support itself. Duerr and his team had also been sounding out at least five manufacturers with a view to pulling in some more subcontract work, and one prospect was Donald Healey, who was keen to get another project going.

In order that production of the Interceptor would not be hamstrung through failure of component supply, Carl Duerr recruited Eric Dancer to handle the buying-in of parts. This was a particularly weak and vulnerable area at Jensen Motors because BMC had previously organized the supply of Healey components for Jensen. So Dancer had to set up virtually the whole system of supply-lines and alternatives in the face of an indifferent parts industry, which was unimpressed by

Jensen's low volumes. Eventually, some firms supplied Jensen simply because of the prestige of the Interceptor.

It also became clear that there were two significant peaks and two notable troughs in the Interceptor's sales pattern, demonstrated by Jensen's accountant and monetary historian Geoff Thompson. It was, of course, necessary to continue at a constant level of production throughout the year, so that delivery times would be consistent.

MARKETING THE INTERCEPTOR

There was no way that a car like the Interceptor could be moved using hard-sell tactics. Such a small-volume high-cost product would appeal more on an emotional level and, as Duerr recognized, the concept of speed and safety has no quantifiable price tag. Much of the marketing effort therefore went into public relations. Quite rightly, it was thought that there were enough people about, fitting into the age range forty-five to sixty, with sufficient funds to buy and run the Interceptor. It was established that this accounted for 80 per cent of Interceptor owners. They felt it would be acceptable to increase prices in 1969 in line with the rest of the industry.

However, increased production meant that there was a need to actually sell cars, where before, every car made was more or less bespoke. The made-to-measure aspect continued, with more and more refinements going into the cars, based on the perceived requirements of owners in the target segment. The Interceptor needed to be fast, comfortable, easy to drive, which meant that everything from steering to windows and air-conditioning had to be powered, plus a four-speaker eight-track stereo. Efforts were made to eliminate wind noise. By 1969 Duerr felt that the Interceptor in the guise of the Mark II was just about right, the 'middle-

Interceptor Series – Specification	
Engine	Mk I and II: Chrysler V8, ohv, 108 × 86mm, 6,276cc, 383cu in, 330bhp @ 4,600rpm. Carter carb. Mk III up to 1973: 300bhp @ 4,800rpm. Holley carb; Carter Thermoquad carb from 1973 on. SP: Chrysler V8, ohv, 109.7 × 95.3mm, 7,212cc, 440cu in, 330bhp @ 4,700rpm. Three Holley carbs. Mk IV 1984–91: 5.9-litre Chrysler V8 with fuel injection.
Transmission	Chrysler Torqueflite 3-speed automatic. Powerlock differential. FF: Ferguson four-wheel drive.
Suspension	Front, independent coil springs and wishbones. Rear, ½ elliptic springs.
Steering	Power-assisted rack and pinion (option on Mk I).
Structure	Box section and tubular steel chassis, welded steel body.
Brakes	Hydraulic dual circuit, servo, 11.25in discs all round. Mk II: Servo, dual circuit, front 11.375in discs, rear 10.75in discs. Mk III: Ventilated discs. FF: Girling, servo, dual circuit, front 11.375in discs, rear 10.75in discs. Maxaret anti-lock system.
Wheelbase	Int: 8ft 9in. FF: 9ft 1in. *Length* Int: 15ft 4.5in. FF: 15ft 11in.

aged executive's dream', and even two-Jensen families were not unknown.

One publicity stunt dreamed up at the time was to turn the Interceptor's interior into an office environment. John Bannenberg, interior designer of the QE2 was commissioned to effect this transformation. The 'Office on Wheels' was unveiled in Harrod's banking department, with such luminaries as Miss World and boxer Henry Cooper, and the stunt generated no less than thirty-five

The most obvious change to the front of the Mark II was the raising of the bumper and placement of sidelights below it.

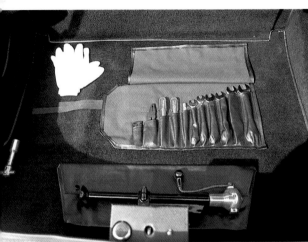

Resplendent in one of those yellow hues popular in the late 1960s, the Mark II Interceptor also features a vinyl roof and Rostyle wheels.

The original Interceptor tool-kit was quite comprehensive, even extending to gloves so as to avoid soiling the interior with dirty fingers after wheel changes.

Hallmark of the Interceptor's back end, the glass hatch was opened by a lever in the driver's door-frame.

The gentleman's luxury carriage stands ready for action: an early 1969 Mark I Interceptor.

column feet of newspaper coverage. But the whole thing would have been far too complex to put into practice, and perhaps rather fortuitously, no one placed an order for their 'Office on Wheels'.

Possibly the most blatant venture into direct selling was the hiring of personable young 'ladies' who were given a thorough briefing on the Interceptor and dispatched into the countryside to offer demonstration runs to key local figures. This still fell under the heading of public relations, since there was no sales pitch, as such, but it did actually result in a number of cars being sold. Schemes very similar to this were common in the US and Japan, where the pretty girl would arrive in the car at the prospective buyer's house and arrange an appointment for the actual salesman to call at a later date.

There were simple publicity measures such as getting the doormen of leading hotels to ensure that Interceptors were to be seen in strategic places, or arranging for prospective customers to visit the factory to see Interceptors in production. Jensen Motors never retained an advertising agency in those days, but they had Tony Good's PR firm and a creative agency which produced brochures, displays and sales literature.

Tony Good remains one of the longest-running players in the Interceptor story: he was Public Relations adviser to Jensen Motors Limited in the early 1960s, joined the board under Carl Duerr, and is still on the International Motors board, as well as running his own PR consultancy.

Anthony Good

Public relations expert Tony Good, aged fifty-seven, is amongst the longest runners in the Jensen saga, for his consultancy Good Relations was retained by Jensen Motors Limited from the early 1960s to advise on presentation and publicity for the new models.

With the involvement of Norcros, his position was, if anything, firmer, and when the Interceptor was launched, he was heavily involved in the marketing operation. When Carl Duerr was moved in as Managing Director, Tony and his ex-Rover press office colleague Gethin Bradley were frequently called in to handle press receptions and impromptu publicity gigs. Bradley was a motoring PR man through and through, whereas Good's expertise lay in the technical and aviation, as well as automotive fields. He also had a financial advisory company called Assets in Action and, together with Duerr, they devised the scheme to sell Jensen Motors from Norcros to merchant bankers Wm. Brandt's Sons. In June 1968, Brandt's took over the whole of the Jensen equity, passing over 38 per cent of it to the Jensen board; this consisted of Duerr, Beattie, Graves, Good, and the bank's nominal Chairman, Welsh.

Whilst recognizing Carl Duerr's undoubted commitment to the Interceptor cause, Tony Good felt that he was too emotionally involved; he accepted everything anyone told him about the cars and the company. To operate a successful PR campaign, he observes, it is vital to have a promotable product and a personable figure at the head of it. However, Duerr, he feels, was something of a self-publicist, perhaps at the expense of marketing man Richard Graves.

Kevin Beattie he recalls as a great person, a very clever engineer, but not particularly streetwise, or given to lateral thinking. Tony Good recalls that he took delivery of a brand new Interceptor, only to find that after only a matter of a couple of weeks, the car had developed tiny rust spots on the bumpers. He showed the car to Carl Duerr, who in turn called in Kevin Beattie. Kevin said it was impossible, as the bumpers were chromed by a firm which coated them to the same specification that they used for chrome-plating taps. And bathroom taps don't rust. Duerr insisted that the bumpers were rusty, and had a pair placed on the factory roof for a week to see what would happen to them. Sure enough, they became rusty. It transpired that the chromers had indeed got access to the tap specification, but, knowing that Jensen had no way of gauging the thickness of the chrome on their bumpers, had simply given them a minimal coating.

When Jensen belonged to Brandt's, Good was looking around for suitable buyers for the company, and they were beginning to export the Interceptor to San Francisco. One of the main dealers there was Kjell Qvale, who had sold something like 10,000 of the 16,000 Austin Healeys exported to the US. As well as the smaller British sports cars, Qvale also sold a few Rolls Royce and Aston Martins, so the Interceptor was a logical car for him to handle. With the death of the Austin Healey, Qvale was anxious to find a replacement, and when it was pointed out to him that the producers of the Interceptor were also the builders of the Austin Healey, he had the idea of a Jensen sports car.

As is told elsewhere, Qvale took over Jensen Motors Limited, brought the Jensen-Healey into production with over-ambitious speed, and was sunk by a precarious deal with Lotus, the world energy crisis and a UK recession. Tony Good meanwhile continued to be a board member of Jensen Motors, transferring to Jensen Parts and Service after the collapse of the main company. He remained on the board until Ian Orford took over, but remained with Bob Edmiston at Britcar Holdings, and is to this day a Director of International Motors and its subsidiaries.

Good Relations continued to expand in the climate of public relations awareness in more strategic, financial and corporate areas, and was the first PR company to go public in 1986. The company, now Good PLC, was acquired by the Low Group in 1986, and Tony Good devolved from the firm in 1989 to set up a small PR firm called Good Consultancy Ltd.

*One of Jensen Motors' own publicity shots of the Convertible, issued by Gethin
Bradley of PR consultants Good Relations, and embargoed for 22 March
1974. Characteristically, it is a good rear-three-quarter view of the car.*

THE CREDIT SQUEEZE

In the winter of 1969–70 Britain was in the
grip of a credit squeeze, and Wm. Brandt's
personnel got cold feet. Based on a backlog of
unsold cars due to the seasonal winter
hickup in the motor trade, amounting to
perhaps £60,000 worth, they decided that
Jensen production levels were overly optimistic and Duerr's plans for privatization were
unrealistic. They insisted on a production cut
back and, although things were under
control as far as Duerr was concerned, it
seemed to be time for him to actively seek out
a buyer for the company. There were at least
twenty possible candidates waiting in the
wings, but the one who appealed most at the
time was Kjell Qvale.

3 The Qvale Era

I remember always wondering how to pronounce his name: phonetically, it's Shell Kervaler. Anyhow, Kjell Qvale, a man of Norwegian descent, had made a fortune after the second World War, dealing in sports cars in southern California where there were plenty of niche markets for different types of car, some of them quite whacky, like beach buggies. California is a rich place, and in the 1950s there was a tradition that when students graduated from High School, their parents would buy them a British sports car. Or Italian, if you go by Dustin Hoffman's Alfa Romeo Duetto in *The Graduate*.

In any case, Qvale, aged fifty-one in 1970, had made his money with MGs and Austin Healeys, but when BMC pulled the plug on the Healey, he spent a couple of years looking around for a replacement. The short-lived MGC, not a bad car in itself, was tagged with the wrong image: a Healey successor it was not. It was suggested to Qvale that he team up with Healey and do a deal with Jensen Motors, which built Healey's cars in the first place, because they were up for grabs. So, in characteristic whirlwind style, in April 1970 he came to Britain, had meetings with Healey, Brandt's and Jensen Motors and, two weeks later, owned the company.

This is over-simplistic, of course. Duerr was a sound man, but despite his unquestionable expertise in communications, he may just have got a little too personally involved with Jensen Motors. He had perhaps failed to get across to Brandt's the potential and enthusiasm which prevailed at Jensen. Surprisingly, only one of Brandt's Directors ever visited the factory; he was Frank Welsh, Chairman of Jensen Motors.

Jensen's credit limit was frozen at a level far too low for a company stripped of capital as part of the original deal, and Brandt's refused to allow Jensen to take up a long-term loan in Swiss francs at the particularly advantageous rate of 8 per cent, insisting that Jensen borrow from Brandt's themselves at 11 per cent, which was 2 per cent over bank-rate interest, and then only up to a set limit. If the limit was exceeded, the annual interest rate would go up to 19.5 per cent. It was obvious that the banking firm was out of touch with the car manufacturer. A dictum from on high, which meant from Lord Aldington, Chairman of National and Grinlay's Bank, who were major shareholders in Brandt's, advised cutting back on overhead expenditure, administration and sales at Jensen, and concentrating on total efficiency and 'proven rate of production to match proven rate of sales'.

Duerr introduced Qvale and Donald Healey to Brandt's, who were presumably delighted to find a buyer, for they immediately issued a press release indicating that Duerr would be moving to head another operation selling Jensen products in Europe. Whether this would have been the right job for Duerr is another matter, for Qvale's first act was to ditch him. It is probable that because Qvale's chief preoccupation was to get the Jensen Healey up and running, whereas Duerr saw Jensen's future with Interceptors, there could be no meeting of minds. Duerr, philosophical but none the less angry, for Brandt's had effectively squeezed him out through raising the capitalization of the company, resigned on 8 May 1970. At least he had the satisfaction of knowing that he had fulfilled his role as 'turnaround man'.

It had always been the intention for Carl Duerr to leave Jensen Motors when the time was right, although the credit squeeze had not been anticipated. Brandt's brought in their own independent management consultant, Alfred Vickers, who had been Deputy Technical Production Manager at Rolls Royce in 1940. To a certain extent, he was seen by Brandt's as fulfilling the same role as Duerr, and after the sell-off to Qvale, Vickers was made Managing Director. His first task was to sack 33 per cent of the workforce, an act which was hardly likely to endear him to the Jensen workforce. Morale was set for a downturn.

The new board consisted of Qvale as President, Donald Healey as Chairman, Geoffrey Healey, Vickers, and the old team of Beattie, Graves and Good. Despite the job cuts, Interceptor production continued to rise to around eighteen units week and, at the close of the 1970–71 financial year, the company had made a £100,000 profit, compared to a loss of around £360,000 during the preceding eighteen months. This is somewhat puzzling when there was meant to have been £1m in the bank in 1968–69.

Left and right: Kevin Beattie and Kjell Qvale, respectively, pose with a new body pressing, with which they appear to be very pleased.

THE JENSEN HEALEY

There was some confusion initially about what the new model should be called: would it be a Jensen, or should it be a Healey, and what of the Lotus engine? Here were three major British names tied together, each one noted for sporting excellence in one field or another, the sales potential of which must have been keenly obvious to Qvale. Carl Duerr had been involved with Donald Healey previously when a suitable engine was sought for the proposed Jensen Healey; having spent a great deal of his working life in Germany, he had a lot of contacts there, amongst which was BMW. He went to see what they might offer for a Jensen Healey project, and they came up with the unit which would power their 2002 Saloon. They also said that it could be warranted from BMW agents worldwide and, what's more, Jensen could have it for a reasonable price. But, as we know, German products are of high quality and are invariably expensive.

BMW were nevertheless prepared to negotiate, but the deal was sacrificed when Qvale dropped Duerr. One of the last things Duerr did was to alert Qvale to the fact that BMW would probably compromise on price, but apparently Qvale decided it would be too expensive, and BMW were not prepared to supply engines in the sort of numbers that he had in mind. So the idea came to nothing. The difference it would have made to the company was incalculable; a reliable, unburstable engine, with warranty and servicing by BMW agents.

Kjell Qvale

It was traditional in the US for proud parents to give their offspring a European sports car when he or she graduated, and it was this climate in particular which brought fame and fortune to Kjell Qvale. Born in 1919, the son of a Norwegian seaman, Qvale had been brought to the US in 1929 and, after the Second World War, he set up in business in San Francisco importing MG sports cars.

During the 1950s and 1960s, he was immensely successful selling Austin Healeys to the Californian graduate set and, by the 1960s, he was trading in Rolls Royce, Aston Martin and Jaguar, as well as other BMC products. The demise of the Healey 3000 was a particularly acute blow to Qvale, because there was little else comparable at the time. As he scouted around for a suitable replacement, his path crossed with Tony Good and Carl Duerr, who were seeking outlets for the Interceptor. About the same time he also met Donald Healey, and once he realized that he had actually been talking to the guys who built the Austin Healey, and their company was potentially for sale, it must have seemed clear to him that here were the seeds of a new Healey sports car.

After meeting with Jensen's owners, Merchant Bankers Wm. Brandt's Sons, in April 1970, Qvale bought out Carl Duerr's holding to become a major shareholder in Jensen Motors Limited; it would not be long before he acquired all of Brandt's shares. The new board at Jensen were all to be minor shareholders, and they included Beattie, Graves, Good, Donald Healey, Geoffrey Healey, and Management Consultant Alfred Vickers, who was to be Managing Director.

Qvale's plan to produce a new Jensen Healey sports car was his stated aim from the outset and, as such, he was not particularly interested in the Interceptor. Appearing at West Bromwich on average twice monthly, having travelled from California via Concorde, Qvale relied on the expertise of his board, and Beattie in particular, to get the Jensen Healey up and running.

The design team for the car was controlled by Beattie, as Chief Engineer, with chassis development by Brian Spicer, and Chassis Engineer Barrie Bilbie on hand from the Healey plant at Warwick, plus Howard Panton to co-ordinate the project. Qvale was keen for the Jensen Healey to have a British engine to go with the William Towns-designed, Jensen-built body, together with its Healey input, and he had been impressed by Lotus's successes on the race circuits. The Lotus-Ford twin-cam was not available, but Lotus were in the throes of developing their new 907 all-aluminium twin-cam unit, based on the single-cam Vauxhall/GM slant-four. Because the engine was very much in its infancy, Lotus's Colin Chapman was reluctant to provide Qvale with guarantees for the engines, and it turned out to be virtually the undoing of Jensen Motors Limited.

In its final incarnation, the Jensen Healey was not a bad car, but there were too many warranty claims from owners suffering from engine oil and fuel leaks; early engines did not have tensioners for the toothed-belt driven camshafts, and in cold weather the belt locked solid as the metal of the alloy engine contracted, with disastrous results. It was to be another five years before the Lotus engine really became good, when it appeared as the 2.2-litre 912 unit in the Eclat series. Jensen had meanwhile ironed out many of the problems.

Qvale's dream had been to produce 200 units a week, and it is perhaps remarkable that within three years of his taking over the company, they were actually building 130 Jensen Healeys a week. It is testimony to the design talents at work at Jensen that at least three new models were under development during this time. When it became clear that the Jensen Healey was draining too much of the company's resources, Qvale decided to throw his marketing acumen behind the Interceptor, and the new Convertible and Coupe versions were introduced.

After Jensen Motors Limited was wound up in May 1976, Qvale's UK business interests centred on his Britcar Holdings company, and he set up Jensen Parts and Service to look after the ongoing interests of Jensen owners. Britcar Holdings, later to become International Motors, was principally involved in the importation of Japanese and Korean cars; Qvale took less of an interest in the affairs now, and finally sold out in 1986 to Bob Edmiston, who had been Financial Controller at Jensen Motors, and Managing Director of Britcar Holdings.

The Jensen-Healey sports car, developed from drawing board to production in just two years. It suffered from numerous mechanical teething troubles and, because of over-ambitious volume production, was largely responsible for bringing the company to its knees.

Qvale was a mass-market man, obliged to stick with the Interceptor, but not that bothered about it for himself. What he really wanted was 200 cars a week, and the Jensen Healey was going to crack it. With its William Towns-styled body compromised by US Federal safety regulations, and majority of stock Vauxhall components, it took two years to progress from conception to the first production model being rolled off the line, which is really fast moving. The Jensen Healey made its début at Geneva in March 1972. Much of the credit must go to Kevin Beattie, although it practically broke him as

THE JENSEN HEALEY			
Mk no.	**Years**	**Engine series**	**Chassis no.**
Mk I	1973–74		10,001 to 13,342
Mk II	1974–76		13,350 to 20,505
GT	1974–76		30,002 to 30,510

Jensen Healey Series – Specification	
Engine	Lotus 4cyl, 2 × ohc, 16 valve, 832 × 84.3mm, 1,973cc, 142bhp @ 6,500rpm. 2-twin choke. Dellorto or Stromberg carbs.
Transmission	Mk I: Chrysler 4-speed manual. Mk II: Getrag 5-speed manual, all synchro.
Suspension	Front: Independent coil spring, double wishbone. Rear: coil spring.
Steering	Rack and pinion.
Structure	All steel, unitary construction. Two door, two seat. GT: Coupe body style.
Brakes	Girling, dual circuit; front 10in discs; rear 9in drums.
Wheelbase	7ft 8in. *Length* 13ft 6in.

he was invariably working an 18-hour day. It is fair to say that the Jensen Healey brought Jensen Motors Limited to its knees.

It was ironic that Qvale bought the engines without any warranty from Lotus. In circumstances verging on the nightmarish, engines were blowing up all over the US. Jensen Motors were faced with masses of litigation suits and, of course, the car gained an evil reputation in its first few months. The engine was certainly underdeveloped, and it acted as a drain on the company because there was no warranty on it. It is a matter of speculation as to whether or not Colin Chapman knew what he was doing. When Jensen stopped using the engine in 1976, having sorted it out once and for all, solving all the gasket failures and oil and petrol leak problems along the way, Lotus began using the engine in all its own models, as they do to this day with the 2.2-litre unit.

As Ian Orford, who later owned the company, observes, 'Chapman picked the engine up after Jensen and its customers had developed it for him, at their expense. You

have to take your hat off to Colin, because he saw an opportunity and Qvale was the patsy.'

When Qvale found the Jensen Healeys weren't selling, he suddenly espoused the Interceptor. Production was pushed up to twenty-five a week and, in fact, he managed to sell rather more in the US. This improved matters financially and it kept things going for a while. Turnover rose dramatically from £3m in 1970 to £14m in 1975. The financial structure of the company was curious, to say the least, as the issued share capital remained at just £60,000; reserves never rose above £250,000, and expansion was always funded through borrowing, at a time of rampant inflation in the UK. Qvale always maintained that 200 Jensen Healeys a week were needed to break even, but the best week's production was 135 units.

Unlike Carl Duerr, who was even to be seen indulging in a game of darts with the men on the shop-floor during their lunch-break, Kjell Qvale was seldom seen at the factory, and remained a distant businessman figure. There was a feeling among the workforce that Jensen Motors Limited in England was being milked. Qvale had also set up Jensen Motors Incorporated in the US, and they bought the cars without warranty from Jensen Motors Limited in the UK. It was never stated how much they were going to pay the factory for making them, so it was thought that the US arm was paying too little. After all, both companies were owned by Qvale; he could therefore pull the strings whichever way he wanted.

It may have been with some justification that the unions pointed out to Qvale that the cars may have been sold to Jensen Motors Incorporated without warranty, but it was clear that they were getting them cheaply; it was also suggested that it was possible for the balance sheet to be adjusted so it would never look good in the UK, and therefore such considerations as wage rises, better terms and conditions of employment were unlikely to be implemented. Whatever was going on has to be reconciled by the old adage 'he who pays the piper calls the tune', and all that.

THREATS TO THE INTERCEPTOR

Jensen Motors had always kept a weather eye on the competition. Perhaps the most obvious challenger was the Bristol, still produced today as the Brigand and Beaufighter and, like the Interceptor, powered by the Chrysler V8. Looking through photographs at Jensens, I came across a picture of a Facel Vega HK500 at the Jensen factory, the last in the line of the French Grandes

The Interceptor Convertible would doubtless have sold well in the US, but its introduction came too late in the Jensen Motors saga. This is a 1974 model, but today, most of Jensen Cars' Mark IVs are built as Convertibles.

Routières under scrutiny by the producers of what might be seen as the British equivalent. However, a new competitor was soon to appear. The day the Jaguar XJ-S was launched in 1974, there was a big meeting at Jensen Motors Limited, for here was a car in the same idiom as the Interceptor, likely to be produced in greater volumes, and with the support of the Jaguar marketing and competition record behind it. It looked set to threaten the one car that was keeping the company solvent. And then within weeks there was the major oil crisis, which proved to be another nail in the Interceptor's coffin in America because of overreaction. Orders for anything over 5 litres were promptly cancelled; petrol was scarce and there were a lot of big-engined cars selling for next to nothing.

THE F-TYPE

At this point, they were still building about twenty-five Interceptors a week, and about 125 Jensen Healeys. Qvale, or Vicker's achievement, was to push Interceptor production up from a regular fifteen, with a much reduced workforce. This was felt by some observers to be tantamount to flooding the market at a time when people were beginning to question the ethics of 13mpg (460km/100l) luxury cars; the men who built them were of the opinion that specifications may have improved, but the actual build quality had fallen.

When sales of the Jensen Healey didn't take off as hoped, Qvale put more pressure behind selling the Interceptors and made a few changes to suit the American market, including different-coloured interiors, and sheepskin-covered seats. With an eye to the Californian climate, no doubt, he introduced the Convertible in 1974, and the Panther-styled Coupe arrived with its brown-tinted glass hoop and XJ-6-derived back window in 1975. Still wrestling with Jensen Healey

*The Jensen Nova was a prototype two-seat grand tourer built in the early
1970s, bearing Italianate as well as US styling influences.*

developments, and the logistics of having to virtually hand-build its GT estate derivative, Kevin Beattie never had time to be involved with designing the Coupe.

In 1973, designs for the Interceptor replacement, known as the F-Type, were commissioned from Ital Design, Bertone and William Towns. By 1975 the Towns-styled car was well on the way to first prototype stage. Displaying contemporary Italianate themes found in cars like the Lamborghini Espada, Giugiaro's Alfa Romeo GTV, and the Lotus Eclat, the F-Type would run with the 7.2-litre Chrysler engine, and it was intended to take Jensen into the luxury-limousine segment typified by the Aston Martin Lagonda.

The G-Model which also made it to prototype stage was going to be a 4-litre intermediate car, falling between the Jensen Healey and the Interceptor, and considerations were being given to ideas for successors to the Jensen Healey. This flurry of activity was going on between 1974–76, and is reminiscent of the desperate thrashing around of a cornered animal which doesn't know which way to turn. Managing Director after Vickers left in 1973, Kevin Beattie was

running himself ragged trying to keep all this under control. All models went down the production line mixed up together.

THE END OF THE LINE

Suddenly Kjell Qvale didn't appear at all. Until mid-1975, he had been coming over on Concorde two or three times a month, sometimes for a couple of days. Then late in 1975, despite efforts to get the Labour government to bale the company out to the tune of £2m, a receiver was appointed. There were also approaches to other manufacturers, but without success.

The official receiver assessed the production methodology, observing that chassis were laid down, panels were fitted and gradually the cars worked their way through paint and trim, electrics and motorizing, down to passing out. The way he set about closing down production was to stop any new vehicles from being started, and anything in-build could progress right the way down the line. This was unfortunate for the men building chassis, for they were the first ones to be made redundant.

The company had until the last car went to sales before it could be sold, or closed down. Throughput at the time was about sixteen weeks, and it took approximately sixteen weeks to sell the car. That represented a great deal of money even to Jensen, which was a big company by specialist car standards, and it was unlikely that a buyer would be found.

The receiver who dealt with the Aston Martin closure simply shut the doors the moment he arrived, and they remained closed for about twelve months. All the workforce went and found jobs elsewhere. Then a consortium bought the company, opened the doors and re-employed the workforce, so they just picked up where they left off. Jensen, on the other hand, didn't have such good fortune. After the last car had gone through, everything had to be sold, basically for whatever it could realize, and things went for next to nothing. Tons of specialist equipment, including jigs, were simply sold for scrap. With hindsight, it should never have happened of course, and some means of putting it into storage should have been devised.

DAWNING OF A NEW ERA

Bob Edmiston arrived in late 1974, as the financial adviser and accountant. He didn't really know much about Jensen, but he was a sound financial man. He saw an opportunity to salvage a little of the company and, indeed, make a little more money than the scrap man would pay. John Griffiths, the receiver, advised Qvale that there was still an obligation to supply spares to Jensen owners in the US. Unlike the sort of *laissez-faire* attitude in the UK, there was a serious possibility of his being sued if there was no such facility in the US, as the cars were still under warranty for brand-new parts. Qvale was advised that it would be in his best interests to buy the new company, Jensen

Bob Edmiston who, as Jensen Motors' Financial Director had the onerous task of bringing in the official receiver in 1975, went on to become Managing Director of Jensen Parts and Service, and later, its holding company, Britcar Holdings. After he sold the Jensen company to Ian Orford in 1982, he developed International Motors into a highly successful organization with several concessions, including Subaru and Isuzu.

Parts and Service Limited, which was ostensibly set up by the receivership.

So Qvale dug deeper into his personal fortune and financed Jensen Parts and Service, placing it under the penumbra of his Britcar Holdings company, and putting shareholder Bob Edmiston in as Managing Director. Qvale also bought the engineering department of the old company which, with all the new models, was an excellent pool of talent. Known as Jensen Special Products, it was set up a couple of miles away from

Jensen Parts and Service, which would operate from the old parts department. The rest of the Jensen Motors factory was sold off and turned into an industrial estate. Jensen Special Products was quickly bought out by its managers, Ray Allsop and Alan Vincent, but it failed in 1986.

Edmiston had visited Japan some eighteen months before the demise of Jensen and had been favourably received by Fuji Heavy Industries, which made Subaru vehicles, and were keen to expand their markets. Now the situation was completely open at West Bromwich, and Edmiston, with a view to maximizing the potential of Britcar Holdings, went back to Fuji, made a deal to import finished cars into the UK, and took on the Subaru franchise.

The deal was that Britcar would do PKD (Part-Knock-Down) work, in which Subarus would arrive from Japan partly assembled and be finished off at Kelvin Way. At the time it was a way for Subaru to circumvent the 11 per cent import quota. Bob Edmiston's

Robert Edmiston

Born in India in 1946, Bob Edmiston spent his childhood in Nairobi, and began his career as a bank clerk in London. Married at the age of twenty, Edmiston earned extra money selling second-hand cars. Then he went to work for Chrysler International as a treasury clerk, moving on to Ford as a financial analyst. Next came a spell as Financial Controller at Automotive Products, before he returned to Chrysler UK in 1970 as a financial manager.

Bob Edmiston's motto was that it is not the length of experience in a job which matters, but the intensity of the experience. His whirlwind career in financial management led him to be appointed Financial Controller and Company Secretary of Jensen Motors Limited in 1974. Kjell Qvale was most impressed by his ambitious manner, but the company was on the downward slope. It was a daunting time to be involved with company finance, for the country was in the grip of a three-day week. He was faced with calling in the receiver, re-negotiating loans, with creditors constantly on the phone, and the shop-floor in turmoil.

When redundancy came in 1976, Bob invested his £600 pay-off, but was immediately asked by Qvale to form the company Jensen Parts and Service Ltd. He took out a loan to add to his redundancy cheque, and acquired a 15 per cent stake in Jensen Parts and Service. After a visit to Japan, Edmiston secured the Subaru franchise for Qvale's Britcar Holdings Company and, in 1977, Subaru UK Ltd was established. The fact that Qvale and Edmiston had only just recovered from a liquidation was sufficient to persuade Subaru parent Fuji industries to give them the franchise; import quotas were uncertain then, and they knew that Britcar Holdings badly needed the Subaru concession.

A new 11-acre site was developed in West Bromwich, and Britcar Holdings moved from the Jensen Parts and Service premises in 1980; by October 1980, a new company known as International Motors was formed, which included a property division. New contracts followed for additional franchises; in 1980 came Maserati and De Tomaso, which were largely unsuccessful due to problems with right-hand-drive supply. Then in 1981 the company took on Hyundai from Korea, and the following year, Edmiston's shareholding increased to 50 per cent. In June 1982 he sold Jensen Parts and Service to Ian Orford, and to all intents and purposes, was no longer a player in the Interceptor story.

In 1986 Edmiston bought out Kjell Qvale to become a major shareholder in International Motors and; by February 1987, Isuzu UK Ltd was officially launched. The following year the parent company became the I.M. Group; its three franchises had sold 23,000 new vehicles in the year.

A free-marketeer, Bob Edmiston has two children, loves water sports and flying; he is a committed Christian, and is now Chairman and Chief Executive of the I.M. Group. He may not have spent a great deal of time at Jensen, but his involvement was crucial at the time of the setting up of Jensen Parts and Service, and in selling the company to Ian Orford, who revived Interceptor production.

reasoning was that in 1976 it wasn't a viable proposition to even think about building a Jensen and, in fact, he didn't really think it ever would be. He could visualize Jensen Parts and Service growing less and less viable and, as the cars became more collectable and did fewer miles, business eventually drying up completely.

Everyone at Jensen Parts and Service was astonished. What were they doing with these peculiar little Japanese cars? To start with, any of the former Jensen dealers who were interested could have first bite of the Subaru cherry, and all Jensen executives were dismissed to knock on garage doors asking if they were interested in the franchise. In this way, no less than forty franchises were picked up around the country, and Kelvin Way was overrun with odd little boxy Mark I Subarus, the first affordable four-wheel-drive cars. The premises were quickly outgrown, and all the Jensens soon disappeared from the workshop because it became the Subaru pre-delivery inspection centre, including the preparation of press cars.

Bemused and disillusioned, what remained of the Jensen workforce could at least be consoled by the fact that the Subarus made a lot of money. The British public kept buying them as fast as they came in. As a consequence, Bob Edmiston needed bigger premises and, in 1981, Britcar Holdings transferred to a new building a few miles away. By now one of the Britcar companies, International Motors, had the franchise for Maserati, De Tomaso and Hyundai cars, and occasionally, the odd Maserati would appear at Jensen Parts and Service for attention to mechanicals, chassis or bodywork.

JENSEN GOES IT ALONE

Bob Edmiston's direction was clearly towards the importation and distribution of the new wave of cars from the Pacific basin. He therefore left Ian Orford as General Manager in charge of Jensen Parts and Service, bearing in mind his continuing enthusiasm for the marque. Orford had two years to wind the place down, with the promise of a job at International Motors. Nobody except Orford knew that that was his brief, otherwise it might have been a different story. He told no one, but during his first six months at the helm, he weighed up the situation and decided that they should make a go of it.

There was sufficient expertise left amongst the forty or so workers, some of whom had been building the Interceptor only a few years earlier. Ian Orford decided that they should concentrate on restoration and, after a small amount of advertising, suddenly the place was crawling with Interceptors whose owners wanted them refurbished. It was Bob Edmiston's turn to be astonished, for this was not what he was expecting. However, he saw that Orford had made the operation viable and offered to sell it to him. From that moment, Orford decided that the goal would be the complete re-manufacture of the Interceptor.

In 1982 a new bodyshell was procured from the depths of a dealer's stores and Albert Mundy's engineering department made a jig from it, as all the original jigs had gone. From then on it was a matter of slowly building the cars. They were virtually identical to the Mark III, except that now they were fitted with a smaller 5.9-litre fuel-injected Chrysler engine, and the front valance sprouted a small air-dam.

SETTING UP THE SUPPLY LINES

After the closure of the company in 1976, it was hard work getting the suppliers to co-operate again because some of the major ones like GKN and Dunlop had actually lost

Albert Mundy

Albert Mundy started with Jensen Motors Limited in 1964, when he was thirty-five, working on the Healey 3000 and Jensen C-V8 lines. 'I thought the Jensen was a fabulous looking car when it first came out. I still think it's a fabulous car. The looks of it aren't dated. With the chassis made like it is, they are really strong. One C-V8 we had in recently for restoration had a head-on collision with a BMW. The BMW didn't drive away but the C-V8 did. The chassis are second to none.'

Too old for an apprenticeship when he joined, he started in the body shop, having always been a sheet-metalworker. For Albert, the Jensen Interceptor was the most interesting car he worked on though. 'The work isn't so difficult, it's the skill that's needed. With an Escort or a Sierra you can get a part and fit it on in a few hours. But with an Interceptor, each individual part has to be made to fit. It was the same when it was built in the old factory over the road. Each car was virtually unique. On each one, the door clearances were lead-loaded up, the panel-gaps are all set in the same way, so each car is in effect an individual although the basic shape is the same.'

'We get a lot of people who've had the cars repaired by other garages who have some of the skills, but just don't get the finish right. We can always tell if the work's been done here. Some restorers just cut the outside sill off and put a new one back on, so it looks good, but it's not welded properly on the inside. We cut it right back into the chassis and weld it as it should be welded. We had one come in not long ago, and the side panel just virtually fell off it. The MOT inspectors just can't tell, because they're not allowed to probe around with screwdrivers to see what's filler and what's solid metal. You can have rust on the inside and not showing on the outside. There's no cure for rust, apart from cutting it out. If a car comes in for restoration, we say it must be stripped to the bare metal.'

'It's more satisfying building a car from scratch. But the panel gaps will still have to be lead-loaded. We are talking about 120 sticks of lead to do one car. The back window is an incredible piece of glass. Triplex make it now, but they used to come from Italy. That was one of Jensen's experiments. I see cars coming back that I remember making in the first place, and some have already been back for resprays or for accident damage to be put right. We've got repair records back to 1970. We have our problems, but we get over them; after all, if we can't fix them, nobody can.'

money. They got something like three pence in the pound from the receiver. To this day, Kent Alloys, part of GKN who made the Mark III alloy wheels, still won't deal with Jensen, although Orford's view was that their best bet was to sell the revived company some more wheels. Kent Alloys had Jensen's tooling for the Interceptor's alloy wheel, and other companies broke up Jensen tooling for scrap, including a huge tool for the Jensen Healey bonnet, which would have at least been useful for restorations.

Jensen Parts and Spares managed to hang on to some of the presses, which are extremely crude looking on the outside. Of course, it is not the outside but the inside which matters. If stored properly with lashings of machine grease on the inside facets, these presses can stand there for years. The most important presses are with people like Motor Panels, where they are used to make the front wings, bonnets, the rear quarters, the bumpers; they remain Jensen property.

GETTING THE MARK IV OFF THE GROUND

There are several big 'ifs' in the Jensen story: If Qvale had pursued the BMW engine deal for the Jensen Healey and not gone all-out for 200 cars a week, the model concerned might not have been a disaster and the firm might not have failed . . . If Ian Orford hadn't been around to start up the Mark IV production, there might well be no new Interceptor today . . .

First stage in the renovation saga: before restoration work can begin, all the car's mechanical components have to be removed.

The period of getting the Mark IV (or Series Four) off the ground was therefore crucial. With Ian Orford at the helm, Jensen were making one car roughly every ten weeks, while trying out different build processes. Eventually, Orford was faced with the catch-22 situation in which he could borrow just enough money to keep himself in control of the business, but not enough to expand the business – a position a lot of companies must find themselves in. If £5m were therefore borrowed, it would simply not be enough to launch a brand-new car and recoup the loan. Thus, Jensen continued to make Interceptors in dribs and drabs *ad infinitum*, but as each new type-approval regulation came along, it was just a matter of marking time.

(Right) The spares department at West Bromwich contains a comprehensive stock of Jensen parts.

Transmission rebuild in progress in the engine shop.

It was going to cost Jensen about £60,000 to get the Interceptor Mark IV type approved, a sum which would be unlikely to be recovered, although this would depend on which cars they were building. New type approvals were introduced that they would have to comply with, which added to the bill, and a loan would be needed to cover this. Jensen weren't able to generate enough cash to renew and update worn-out tooling which would have made parts cheaper and, therefore, the cars less expensive. Some of the present Jensen tooling goes back to 1967; thus increasingly more lead is used on the cars in manufacture, as well as more handwork to get the cars into shape.

The name Jensen Parts and Service literally meant that, as a parts and service outfit, a lot of components and equipment off the tracks were inherited. As Parts Manager at the time, Ian Orford recalls that they seized anything they could lay their hands on, as there would be no compromises after the doors finally shut on the main factory. From the point of view of continuing to build the cars, it proved to be a shrewd move. However, in retrospect, it gave an erroneous idea of the cost of producing a car, as a proportion of the components was acquired at no cost. Eventually though, these 'free' parts would be used up and would have to be accounted for; Orford therefore calculated the cost of these as about 20 per cent of the total cost of the Mark IV they were building. Thus, after selling say fifty cars, he would be looking at the true unit cost.

At the time, the classic car market wasn't as influenced by price rises as it is today, so it

Ian Orford

Ian Orford was born in 1945 and joined Jensen in 1968, having been a Jaguar mechanic. He joined the parts department as a materials controller, chasing up suppliers on the phone. By 1974 he was Parts Manager, and remained so until being made redundant in 1976. He was re-employed in the same position almost immediately when the new company, Jensen Parts and Service, was set up.

'I wanted to try something different from the shop-floor anyway, and I thought the parts side would also give me a taste for parts production. I didn't like the way things were going in the factory, and from the Parts division I could watch the whole thing from a distance. Nevertheless, I was made redundant the same as everybody else. Before the closure, the unions and Qvale went to the Labour government as a combined force to ask for assistance. Jensen Motors Limited wanted £2m to pay off all the debts, and about £6m to get the company back on the road. The jobs of 1,800 men hung on it. The government had just given £74m to Chrysler UK, who sold it all off two years later. I've always thought it was purely personal, that a Labour government is never going to give handouts to a firm building a car for the *nouveau riche* and the wealthy, a company owned by an American as well. It's all so obvious in retrospect, but at the time we couldn't understand why they wouldn't save these jobs. After all, they were paying 50 per cent of the redundancy money.'

'I think Qvale had just so much money on one side that he was prepared to lose, but his personal fortune was going to remain untouched. In fairness, I think I'd probably be the same. You have your family's future to protect. I think he always thought we had let him down as well. We hadn't come up with the production volumes he wanted, and the Jensen Healey had been so much trouble in the early days. But a lot of what he was asking was untenable; he wasn't a car man, and he didn't understand the car business.'

'I was re-employed along with about seventy other people by Bob Edmiston and ostensibly Qvale under the Britcar Holdings banner, which was one of Qvale's companies. When Bob Edmiston left me in charge of what was left of the Jensen operation, I thought it was worth giving it a go, so we did some advertising and lo and behold Jensen owners flocked in because they had nowhere to take their cars to get them serviced or re-fettled. I remember Bob coming down one day, and it just knocked his eyes out to see so many Jensens being worked on. He could see these new parts which I had ordered arriving, and I pointed out that he had given me two years to do more or less what I wanted. He saw that I could make some money out of it if nothing else, and within about a week he came back and offered to sell me the company. I re-mortgaged my house, and I had to stump up as much as I could afford, and the bank took a lien on everything else. And I took the plunge. Then it was a matter of working steadily towards getting the Mark IV up and running.'

'One of the things which could have set the Interceptor up as a really special car was the Hemi engine. The Chrysler 440 is a big, fairly crude cast-iron lump. But in its more refined forms it is a heck of an engine. My argument was that there's everything out there now to buy and build our own engine blocks, put together by specialists. If you are going to sell this car for £100,000, each customer should know that someone has specially made the engine. The irony to me is that one of the smallest manufacturers in the world uses the most mass-produced engine, the small-block Chevy. So Jensen is still not going to get away from the truck engine syndrome. The people buying these cars are specialist enthusiasts, so why not give them an enthusiast's engine?'

was hard to evaluate markets and figure out how to obtain the current type approval which, after all, would only be UK approval. Even now, the Mark IV hasn't got full EEC or US Federal approval. Orford couldn't see the company as being in a position to retool, procure parts cost-effectively and get full Federal type approval, let alone update the car in essential areas such as providing more leg-room at the back and a hood which went down flush with the rear bulkhead, and doing something about the rear-quarter-light windows, which were on a perplexing 90-degree elbow-hinge system. There was just too much for a small company to do without being able to generate more money.

Orford looked around and put out feelers to find an interested person. Initially, he sought a silent partner who could invest a couple of million to help the business over some of the hurdles and on to the next step up, which would be new tooling and modern type approval, and perhaps even full EEC type approval. Once the cars started to sell, the cash would accumulate and progress would be easier.

GAINING TYPE APPROVAL

A car does not necessarily have to be in a collision to acquire type approval. Type approval works as a matrix of twenty-three sections, each requiring a minister's approval that the car fulfils the required standard in that section. For instance, for the section on tyres (in fact, the easiest of all), if VR-rated tyres are fitted, they need not be checked at all, as they are a top-rated tyre; if, however, HR-rated tyres were fitted which are only certified up to 130mph (210kph), then approval would have to be obtained. This amounts to a 24-hour test to make sure the tyres will not burst. A critical area is steering column movement on a 30mph (50kph)-frontal impact. The car has to be crashed and the steering column movement measured. Quite obviously, the car will be written off.

Another area is that of emissions, where the car has to have a bag test. The engine is started and for about half-an-hour the emissions from the tail pipe are collected and then analysed. The car has to be set up so that the CO and NO levels meet regulations, a very expensive test. Engine noise is measured by driving past a decibel meter at 30mph (50kph) top gear. As you go by in second gear, you change to top. For the brake test, Jensen did their sums first, and fitted a new anti-lock valve.

For a company as small as Jensen, one of the hardest tests to comply with was for the glass, which had to correspond with the modern new markings. A big company like the Rover Group or Jaguar would have no problem here, because Triplex, for instance, would be only too happy to provide a complete set of glass for a new prototype, all marked up properly at short notice. But they would not necessarily be so keen to do the same for a company like Jensen. In the event, Triplex came up with acid markings, so that Jensen could acid-mark existing glass, which was perfectly legal because Triplex could verify that the glass would pass that test.

There are some big tests like external and internal projections. All external projections must pass a 5mm radius, so that there are no sharp edges to injure pedestrians. This means, in effect, rounding off all protrusions. For the test, a head-shape is fitted into spaces like that over the bumper or to one side of the overrider, and anything it touches has to meet the 5mm radius. This applies all over the car and, for Jensen, one of the most absurd places was the inside top edge of the rear number-plate light, closest to the back panel of the car. It proved just possible to get a head-shape down there, so they had to change the light. Door handles had to be changed, and badges had to be recessed.

SALVAGE

National type approval started in the UK on 1 October 1978. Manufacturers were not expected to change a model midway; if a car was in current production, the manufacturer could keep that model going without type approval, provided one or two updates were made, such as windscreen wipers. That is why the Mini and the Morgan, which were being built long before 1978, are still being produced. As long as these aren't altered, they can continue to be produced. However, Jensen were caught up in the predicament

The Interceptor and FF's distinctive rear screen was made by Triplex; a heating element was essential to combat condensation in temperate climates.

in so far as they stopped production of the Interceptor in 1976. When they tried to resume production in 1982–83, they were advised that type approval would be necessary.

When the parent company was in receivership in 1976, a great deal of material from the factory was disposed of. It is sad to reflect that this included literally hundreds of trophies and medallions that had been won over the years for bodywork or engineering achievements. All the receiver was interested in was what he could sell, and it was a heartbreaking time for most of the workforce. Ian Orford managed to salvage shoeboxes full of engineering photographs and production data, which he perceived as too important to lose. 'It was like a cash and

carry,' he recalled, 'you grabbed them, and you only had one chance.'

Amongst this material there chanced to be some 35mm film, which turned out to be of the crash-testing of the Interceptor which was carried out in 1970 so it could be sold in the US market, where regulations were far more advanced than those of Europe. So, when Ian Orford was faced with crash-testing for UK type approval in 1982 to get the Interceptor production going again, they got the film processed on to VHS video and presented it to the Department of Transport. The Department studied it and, knowing how much a crash-test would cost Jensen, said it was acceptable for the UK regulations. This decision was also based on original telexes between the DoT, MIRA and the US Type Approval board, declaring the Jensen crash-test was about the best they had ever seen.

A steering column is permitted 5in movement towards the driver; the Interceptor's column had moved less than an inch. Thus the DoT said that as long as the cars were built the same, there was no need to get the steering column tested. They also noted that there were no wrinkles in the roof, nor the door panels or frames and, although the screen had come out, there were no wrinkles in the sheet metal. They were therefore happy to accept that it was the chassis which took all the impact, making it quite acceptable for Jensen to build the Convertible.

There was one further snag. Ian Orford argued that the disputed fascia panel did not need to be changed, since anyone wearing a seat-belt would not strike it. The Department of Transport rejected this argument on the basis that a passenger had to come out of the seat-belt, and the retardation of the fascia panel had to meet standard criteria. The Jensen fascia panel was originally three fibreglass pieces fitted together and covered with a dense foam and then leather trim. Once the head had hit the leather and foam, it would hit the fibreglass.

This test cost Jensen £6,000. The retardation was measured as a graph by hooking up the fascia to a machine. At first, there was no retardation whatsoever, implying that the passenger's head was flattened. The driver's side, with the steering wheel separating the driver from the fascia, did not have to conform. Finally Jensen drilled holes in the fibreglass until it resembled a Swiss cheese, which was approved of. Thus the Interceptor passed all the tests to get full UK type approval, something a lot of people said they would never manage to do.

LAUNCH OF THE MARK IV

The new Mark IV (or Series Four) Interceptors were first seen at the Birmingham Motor Fair in 1983, and were launched

A Mark IV Convertible bodyshell in primer has just left the factory spray booth.

Left: Pat Skidmore working on the inner wing section of the first of the Mark IV Convertibles just before it leaves the main body jig.

Ian Orford with the Mark IV Convertible at the Interceptor's relaunch at the Earls Court Show in 1984. Ian was later critical of the stand's low profile presentation, feeling that a more opulent demonstration would have engendered more confidence in the new company.

Having redesigned the rear-end of the car and produced new wings and conventional boot-lid to suit, Jensen launched the Convertible in March 1984. This is an early production line shot.

officially at the 1984 Earls Court Motor Show. Ian Orford had a Convertible and a Saloon on display, priced around £40,000. Charles Folletts, who had sold Jensens since the pre-war days from their plush Mayfair showrooms, and probably sold more Interceptors than anyone else, said they wanted the first twelve cars. At the time they did not know it, but Jensen had only built the two cars on display. Folletts wanted only Convertibles; in return for selling them they wanted sole UK distributorship.

This was therefore quite a startling opening to the proceedings at the show which was otherwise something of a disappointment. While a lot of people were interested in the Jensen vehicles, there was still the prevailing impression that the company was bankrupt. A lot of hard-headed businessmen came along, claiming to have been Jensen owners previously and admiring the Mark IV, but promising to come back in two years time if Jensen were still in business.

It was a tough lesson for Orford. They did not have a decent brochure and they had a poor position in the Earls Court hall because they could not afford anything better. There was no hospitality lounge and none of the trappings which make a company look credible – only a corner stand, a fridge and a telephone. Porsche, Mercedes and Jaguar, of course, wooed the customer in a completely different way, making Orford realize that manufacturing cars and selling them was like chalk and cheese.

Despite a steel workers' strike in Germany and no cars to sell, Porsche still had a stupendous stand at the Motor Show costing £250,000, staffed with pretty girls providing drinks, and a hospitality lounge for their dealers. Said Orford: 'It's highly

Proportions of the Interceptor Convertible are close to perfection, whether the top is down . . .

. . . or up.

Because of the large area of fabric with the hood closed, rear three-quarter vision in the Convertible can be quite a problem.

Convertibles are beautifully upholstered; however, hood stowage necessitates a somewhat ungainly hump behind the rear seats.

The Convertible has a leaner look than the Interceptor saloon.

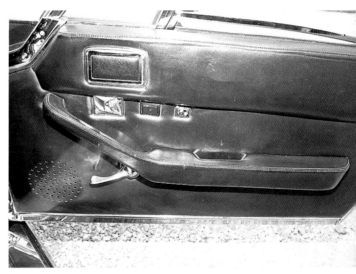

Sweeping door-pull and arm rest complement Convertible door trim, which also accommodates minor switchgear; the window frames lower right into the door.

Wind-in-the-hair motoring as stylish as you can get.

Air-conditioning controls and automatic shift on the Convertible's console.

*Displaying a goodly amount of chrome, stainless steel and hand-finished
paintwork, the Interceptor Convertible looked at home in any setting.*

professional, the gin and tonic end of the
market. It's totally divorced from production, type approval or anything else. You
need someone with tunnel vision for selling,
and a good big budget.'

SELLING UP

In April 1984, Ian Orford had an 80 per cent
stake in the company and his two co-directors, Bruce Collard (Parts Director) and
Chris Lord (Company Secretary/Account-
ant), had 10 per cent each. It was in this year
that Hugh Wainwright first arrived on the
scene, visiting Jensen to enquire about
buying a car. Not being able to afford a Series
Four at this stage, he asked what he could
get as an alternative. Orford suggested that
Wainright could buy a second-hand Mark III
which he would fully restore for him. At the

time this cost about £15,000. During the
period of the restoration, the two men formed
a mutual liking; Wainwright was obviously
a successful businessman, which gave him
great credibility.

Then, about three years later, Orford had
an approach through Wainwright's solicitor
to ask if he was interested in selling the
company. At the time, Orford was negotiating with another party, and delayed respond-
ing to Wainwright. The first deal falling
through, he began talks with Wainwright.
Orford thought Wainwright seemed to be the
right man to consult with, as he was very
enthusiastic about the market, and very
ambitious.

In 1987, the company's name changed to
the more logical Jensen Cars Limited. Ian
Orford sold the company on 1 January 1988,
staying on as Director, which quickly
became Production Director, then Pro-

duction Manager; the result was his resignation. Ian Orford was the victim of the ongoing cycle where newer talents and skills displace older ones; it's perfectly obvious that in such a situation one might as well get out, as the pressures are totally unacceptable.

Orford was simply glad to leave in the end, for it had all gone wrong for him. He was concerned that there was nobody left with enough knowledge of the motor industry to create the new car. Some people with experience only in the tuning business have swiftly come and gone during the last two years, but Orford feels that Chairman Wainwright has yet to meet the right man to be his Production Manager: 'There's just a chance that someone could come in, take it by the scruff of the neck, have 100 per cent authority over it, and make something of it.' Orford suggests a scenario for the new model:

There would have to be new tooling if you are sure that the parts you make are going to be carried through. So for the updated Mark V, the front wings are going to have to be redesigned, but maybe the door skins, part of the rear quarters could be carried through, so it is worth spending money on those. There would need to be updated tools, so that the presses could be used for all the old model spares and the new model. You have to compromise, making it as cost effective as possible.

Sad to say, perhaps the two most significant figures of the Interceptor days are no longer with us – Kevin Beattie, ill and physically exhausted, died in 1975, aged only forty-eight; while Carl Duerr, sprightly and active to the end, died in 1988. Beattie's was the engineering vision which created and perpetuated the Interceptor, whilst Duerr's manner of running the company and divining the right niche and marketing approach for the car ought to have been appropriated, and with more perspicacious backing, might well have prevailed.

4 Specification of the Interceptors

PROBLEMS WITH VIGNALE

From the outset, Interceptor manufacturer was never plain sailing, for there were serious flaws in the earliest Italian-built cars. They were regarded as an embarrassment when they first came out. Every one of the first sixty cars made by Vignale was recalled, although some escaped this and were never returned for rectification and modification. There were said to have been about five lists of modifications, including repaint and finish. It seems Vignale had applied a lot of thick filler paint with the result that there was a lot of cracking on the surface, while any panels covered with trim had not been painted in the belief that the trim stuck better on the bare metal.

The basic specification was there, which was obvious, for the chassis was based directly on the C-V8, but the cars supplied by Vignale were disappointing by any standards and certainly as far as Beattie and the ruling elite were concerned. There were also problems with panel-fit and scant attention was paid to rust protection. It was some time before the Jensen workforce had put matters right. It was therefore decided to terminate the arrangement with the Italian company, and the contract was concluded with a cash payment when the jigs and presses were imported to West Bromwich.

The techniques for building a complex car like the Interceptor from the beginning were quite familiar to the majority of the workforce, already well used to building Healeys, Tigers, and Volvos, as well as the different disciplines of making fibreglass bodies. However, the unions were not happy with the lack of demarcation in the build process because several people's functions overlapped, and a certain amount of negotiation was necessary to overcome this issue.

It is perhaps surprising that the ruling Jensen hierarchy had not learned their lesson from assembling the P1800 Volvo, for which the Linwood-Pressed Steel panels had been less than satisfactory. The Jensens themselves would very probably have said, 'We told you so', since they were never in favour of the Italian contribution in any case. However, these difficulties were resolved, and Carl Duerr and his marketing team of PR men, Tony Good, Gethin Bradley, and ex-Rolls Royce man Richard Graves, set about moulding the Interceptor into a desirable commodity. By the middle of 1969, some seventeen cars were being produced each week, and sales were booming.

MECHANICAL SPECIFICATION

Since the Interceptor was virtually the same car as the C-V8 but with a steel body, it was no surprise that the 6,276cc Chrysler V8 engine was retained, together with the three-speed Torqueflite automatic gearbox. During the Interceptor's early years, the engine and gearbox were being uprated by Chrysler, and no fewer than five different configurations

A new Interceptor starts life on the jig of the West Bromwich bodyshop; steel plates are welded on individually.

were available; these are manifest as V, B, C, D, and E.

The quality of Jensen's fundamental engineering was very good, so the transmission which was selected could cope more than adequately with the V8's 325bhp and hefty 425lb (192.8kg) per ft of torque. The Powr-Lok limited-slip differential was fitted, with a final-drive ratio of 3.07:1. Armstrong Selectaride rear dampers were used, with dashboard control but, in practice, on a reasonably good road, little difference could be discerned between the number 1 soft setting and the number 4 hard setting. On a poor road surface, however, it was possible to compromise with the potholes and achieve a softer but less acute ride, fine for a leisurely journey, but dangerous if wanting to press on.

The Mark II's Rostyle wheels had painted rims rather than chromed.

Jensen still use the GKN pattern five-spoke alloy wheel, and this one is shod with a 225/70 × 15 Dunlop SP Sports radial, a far cry from the original Rostyles and cross-plies.

At this stage Jensen were still putting their money on cross-ply tyres, perhaps because they gave a more comfortable ride, but the Dunlop RS5s which were standard fitment were prone to aquaplane over 120mph (195kph). Although radial-ply tyres were an option, this archaic situation was put to rights in 1969, when the rim size of those common late 1960s Rostyles was increased from 5 to 6in. Rims were simply silver-painted rather than chromed. Not until 1971 would the Interceptor get the wheels it deserved – the far more attractive five-spoke GKN 6.5in alloy rims – and Dunlop SP Sport radials were mercifully introduced in 1969, going over to GR70 profiles on the GKN rims. The servo-assisted

Dunlop Maxaret brakes were employed to bring the Interceptor to heel and, under normal circumstances, were quite adequate, being progressive in action. But, under really severe pressure, they could vibrate noisily and die.

SUSPENSION SET-UP

Suspension for all models was similar; the front assembly used double wishbones with coil springs, dampers and anti-roll bar, whilst the rear consisted of semi-elliptic dual-rate leaf springs, with rubber-button inter-leaved separators; there were Armstrong telescopic dampers and a Panhard rod. The standard of ride and handling was excellent for its day, and not at all bad in 1991, considering the somewhat antiquated leaf-spring back end. To describe riding in the Interceptor in everyday terms, the impression is that of being in an oversized 3-litre Capri, Scimitar GTE, or perhaps even an MGB GT.

LEAKS

There were some problems with the Mark I Interceptors concerning leaking. The major fault seems to have been with the screens not fitting properly, so that rainwater would run between the rubbers and build up under the seats. The Healey suffered the same problem, and there were those who said you could never stop a Healey from leaking. Sports cars are always a problem, but the Interceptor was meant to be a different kind of car which comfortably protected its occupants from any intrusion of the elements.

Oddly enough, there was never any trouble in this respect with the FF. It may have been the different chassis layout, or perhaps just that a little more care was taken in building the sill. The sill on the FF is an out-rigger tube running straight along the outside of the car. The round part of the tube is actually inside the car, whereas that of the regular Interceptor simply consisted of block sections fitted together, which allowed water, if it got in, to seep into the car.

FLEXIBLE MANUFACTURING

Being a small company also allows for much more flexibility, and Jensen were able to streamline the build operation by making minute changes to the procedure. The disadvantage of this slightly haphazard methodology was that nobody bothered to log the changes. As the days went by, they found it

The Jensen badge on the Mark I's C-pillar ventilator is the only identification on the side.

made sense to eliminate or modify certain minor aspects of the car, such as the front quarter lights, which would no longer open. The Jensen badge on the hefty 'C' pillar was transformed into an air-extractor vent. The Interceptor also got a smaller-diameter steering wheel, and power assistance became standard. In a move which paralleled Jaguar's with their new XJ-6, the Dunlop-brake calipers gave way to Girling ones, which required less effort to work and were less inclined to fade. The front suspension was revised to include top and bottom ball-joints and telescopic dampers, avoiding the old Sheerline-derived king-pin and lever-arm damper arrangement. By 1969, the wheels and particularly the tyres had been updated, and in October of that same year when production of Interceptors stood at 1,033 cars with another 196 FFs, it was decided to bring in the Mark II series.

VISUAL DIFFERENCES

The most obvious visual difference between a

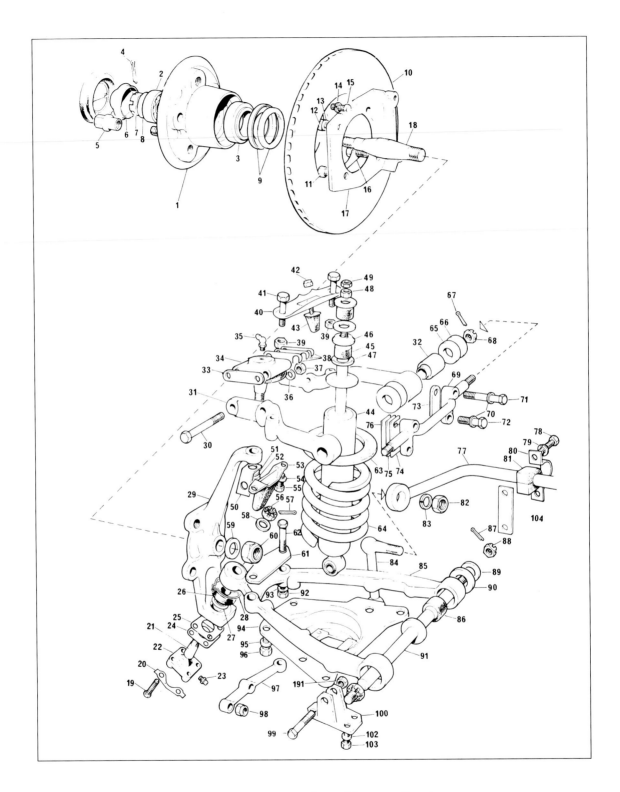

The Interceptor's independent front suspension was by wishbones, coil springs and telescopic dampers. The vital anti-roll bar can be seen at centre right. Hub assembly included ventilated brake discs.

1	Hub c/w studs and bearing cups		ball joint		rubber	80	Strap – mtg. – anti-roll bar
2	Bearing – hub – outer assy	29	Vertical link	54	Washer – spring	81	Mounting rubber – anti-roll bar
3	Bearing – hub – inner assy	30	Bolt – ball joint to upper wishbone outer/inner)	55	Screw	82	Nut
4	Split pin – hub nut	31	Arm – upper wishbone assy – front RH/rear LH	56	Nut – slotted	83	Washer – spring
5	Nut – wheel			57	Split pin	84	Link – anti-roll bar RH/LH
6	Cap – hub	31	Arm – upper wishbone assy – front LH/rear RH	58	Washer – plain	85	Lower wishbone arm assy
7	Nut – hub			59	Washer – plain		
8	Washer – hub nut	32	Bush – rubber	60	Nut – nyloc	86	Bush – lower wishbone arm
9	Seal assy – oil	33	Distance piece – joint to link	61	Plate – platform – bump	87	Split pin
10	Brake – disc	34	Ball joint – upper	62	Bolt	88	Nut – slotted
11	Bolt – caliper adaptor plate	35	Grease nipple – ball joint	63	Insulator – front coil spring	89	Washer – plain
12	Screw – caliper adaptor plate	36	Washer – plain	64	Spring – front coil	90	Washer – prescollan
13	Washer – spring	37	Nut – nyloc	65	Washer – inner	91	Shaft – lower fulcrum
14	Washer – spring	38	Packing piece	66	Washer – prescollan	92	Nut – lock
15	Bolt	39	Nut – nyloc	67	Split pin	93	Washer – plain
16	Washer – tab	40	Bracket mtg. – rebound rubber	68	Nut – slotted	94	Pan – front spring assy RH/LH
17	Plate – cable adaptor RH/LH	41	Bolt	69	Shaft – upper fulcrum		
18	Stub axle	42	Nut – nyloc	70	Washer – spring	95	Washer – spring
19	Bolt – ball pin to link	43	Rebound rubber	71	Bolt – fulcrum shaft	96	Screw
20	Washer – tab	44	Shock absorber – front	72	Bolt – fulcrum shaft	97	Arm – steering side RH/LH
21	Ball pin – lower	45	Stem bush	73	Spacer – fulcrum zero-chamber	98	Nut – nyloc
22	Cap and socket assy	46	Supporting washer	74–6	Plate – packing	99	Bolt
23	Grease nipple – cap and socket	47	Retaining washer	77	Anti-roll bar	100	Bracket – mtg. – shock absorber
24	Shim 0.002in	48	Nut	78	Screw	101	Nut – nyloc
25	Shim 0.004in	49	Nut-lock	79	Washer – spring	102	Washer – spring
26	Gaiter – rubber – ball joint	50	Bracket – support RH/LH brake hose			103	Screw
27	Retainer – gaiter – ball joint	51	Washer – plain			104	Spacer – anti-roll bar
28	Clip – gaiter –	52	Nut – nyloc				
		53	Stop – bump				

Mark I and a Mark II car is the location of the front bumper. It is 2in (50mm) higher than the original car's, the overriders are rectangular instead of being pointed, and the side lights and indicator units swap places with the bumper. Overriders were changed at the back, naturally, and a lever in the offside door-shut substituted for the knob which opened the rear greenhouse hatch. The bumper was not raised for cosmetic reasons: US safety regulations required bumpers to be of a particular height off the ground, and Jensen were not alone in rising to the challenge, which in the case of the MGB and the Porsche 911, did the cars no favours at all aesthetically.

Under the bonnet, the cylinder heads got aluminium rocker covers emblazoned with the Jensen logo, and a revised wiring loom now took twelve fuses. Instead of an ammeter, there was now a voltometer for checking battery condition, and hazard warning lights were incorporated into the indicator circuit.

Tank capacity was increased by four gallons so that, in theory, the Interceptor II's 20 gallons (160 litres) gave it a range of about 320 miles (510km). You didn't have to bother with the key to open the petrol cap any more; a switch on the redesigned dashboard did the trick. These remote control switches are fine until pressed by mistake; the worst one is opening the boot when you meant to adjust the driver's seat. Fortunately, the Interceptor never presented that problem. A further safety feature was the collapsible

Jensen's own publicity shot of the Mark II car neglects to include the appropriate grille badge; it should say Interceptor II. The driving lights were an option which was quite frequently adopted.

The Mark II Interceptor was launched at the Earls Court Motor Show in October 1969, and the main visual difference was in the raising of the front bumper; the sidelight-indicator units were now set below the bumper, and the overriders were squared off.

Flat, pointed overriders and these particular light clusters show this to be a Mark I car; GB plate indicates it has either already been or is about to be used for some foreign expedition.

The fascia of the Mark II cars was heavily revised from the more sporting layout of the Mark I. It could be described as plain, simple and elegant, using rocker switches instead of the earlier toggle variety. The ignition switch was now located on the steering column.

1	Forward harness	4	Switch panel harness	7	Interior light
2	Body harness	5	Door harness – RH		harness
3	Fascia panel harness	6	Door harness – LH		

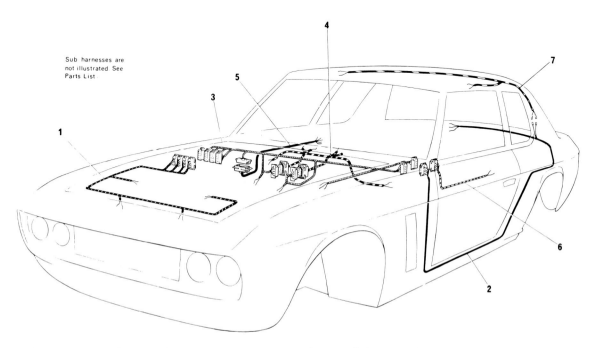

Sub harnesses are
not illustrated See
Parts List

*The main wiring loom in the Interceptor, consisting of forward, fascia and
body harnesses, follows logical paths. Sub-harnesses such as those for
headlamps and indicators, plus auxiliaries like the aerial are more
complicated and link up with the main harnesses.*

steering column, and the dash now incorporated rocker rather than toggle switches,
placed in a row, keyboard style, above the radio
on the central console. The auxiliary gauges
were all in individual nacelles above the
switchboard and angled towards the driver.

DEMISE OF THE FF

By 1969, sales of the FF were not going well,
in spite of the universal enthusiasm for the

*(Left) Mark II set to spring into action; nose-
up, tail-down attitude achieved by suspension
settings, coupled with angles of door pillars.*

technology it represented. The fact that
nobody had enjoyed much success with a four-
wheel-drive car in competition perhaps made
buyers hold back, for its full potential was
still an unknown quantity. In sales terms, it
was useless in the export stakes, because the
design of the front drive-train made no
allowance for converting to left-hand drive. A
crude attempt was tried using a chain-drive
system, but this was too impractical. Also,
potential owners couldn't be lined up at the
drop of a hat for test drives and demon-
strations when the snow came. So, it was
decided to end production and concentrate on
a face-lift of the basic Mark II Interceptor and,
at the same time, create a new prestige model.

ROAD TEST
Jensen Interceptor (6,276 c.c.)

Reproduced from *Autocar*

MANUFACTURER
Jensen Motors Ltd., Kelvin Way, West Bromwich, Staffordshire.

PRICES

Basic	£3,980	0	0
Purchase Tax	£1,218	8	0
Total (in G.B.)	£5,198	8	0

EXTRAS (inc. P.T.)

Stereo radio/player	£71	16	2
Radial ply tyres . . .	£20	11	3
Price as tested	£5,290	15	5

PERFORMANCE SUMMARY

Mean maximum speed	137 mph
Standing start ¼-mile	15.0 sec
0–60 mph	6.4 sec
30–70 mph through gears	6.2 sec
Typical fuel consumption	14 mpg
Miles per tankful	225

At-a-glance: Latest version of British GT with Italian styling and American engine. Lots of performance; light fade-free brakes; very smooth transmission. Power steering. Handling normally good. Nicely trimmed. Needs better ventilation.

The recovery of Jensen Motors from a very shaky position in 1966 has been something of an industrial marvel. New management and a good product have been responsible, and Jensen now rates as number one in the specialist car field. Over 1,200 Interceptors and FFs have been made in only 2½ years and production is now averaging 17 cars per week. In the light of this we decided it was time to reappraise this exciting American-engined GT.

It was 5 January 1967 when we first tested the Interceptor with its Chrysler 6.3-litre vee-8, Torque flite automatic transmission, conventional suspension and beautiful Vignale body. Since then there have been detail changes to the engine (better torque and

Very few manufacturers were bold enough to use such a vast expanse of glass to finish the rear of the design; in the mid-1960s it was thought most dashing.

ACCELERATION

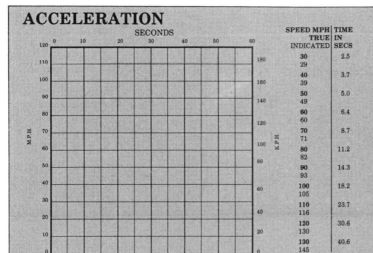

SPEED MPH TRUE INDICATED	TIME IN SECS
30 / 29	2.5
40 / 39	3.7
50 / 49	5.0
60 / 60	6.4
70 / 71	8.7
80 / 82	11.2
90 / 93	14.3
100 / 105	18.2
110 / 116	23.7
120 / 130	30.6
130 / 145	40.6

SPEED RANGE, GEAR RATIOS AND TIME IN SECONDS

mph	Top (2.88)	Inter. (4.17)	Low (7.06)
10–30	–	2.5	2.6
20–40	3.4	2.7	2.1
30–50	3.5	2.8	2.6
40–60	4.1	3.3	–
50–70	5.0	4.3	–
60–80	6.0	5.0	–
70–90	6.8	5.6	–
80–100	7.8	–	–
90–110	9.9	–	–

PERFORMANCE

MAXIMUM SPEEDS

Gear	mph	kph	rpm
Top (mean)	137	186	5,100
(best)	137	186	5,100
Inter.	95	153	5,100
Low	55	88	5,100

BRAKES

(from 70 mph in neutral)
Pedal load for 0.5g stops in lb

1	45	6	35
2	40	7	35
3	37	8	35
4	35	9	37
5	33	10	40

RESPONSE (from 30 mph in neutral)

Load	g	Distance
10 lb	0.12	251 ft
30 lb	0.42	72 ft
50 lb	0.92	33 ft
60 lb	0.98	30.7 ft
Handbrake	0.30	

Max. Gradient 1-in-5 (see text)

MOTORWAY CRUISING

Indicated speed at 70 mph . . . . 71 mph
Engine (rpm at 70 mph) . . . . 2,650 rpm
(mean piston speed) . . . 1,495 ft/min.
Fuel (mpg at 70 mph) . . . . 18.3 mpg
Passing (50–70 mph) . . . . 3.7 sec

COMPARISONS

MAXIMUM SPEED MPH

Monteverdi 375L	152	(£10,250)
Aston Martin DBS	140	(£6,112)
Jaguar E-type 2+2	139	(£2,642)
Jensen Interceptor	**137**	**(£5,198)**
Porsche 911E	130	(£4,243)

0–60 MPH, SEC

Monteverdi 375L	6.3
Jensen Interceptor	**6.4**
Jaguar E-type 2+2	7.4
Aston Martin DBS	8.6
Porsche 911E	9.8

STANDING ¼-MILE, SEC

Monteverdi 375L	14.6
Jensen Interceptor	**15.0**
Jaguar E-type 2+2	15.4
Aston Martin DBS	16.3
Porsche 911E	17.0

OVERALL MPG

Porsche 911E	19.0
Jaguar E-type 2+2	18.8
Jensen Interceptor	**12.9**
Aston Martin DBS	12.7
Monteverdi 375L	11.6

TEST CONDITIONS: Sunny. Wind: 0 mph. Temperature: 25 deg. C. (77 deg. F). Barometer: 29.95 in hg. Humidity: 40 per cent. Surfaces: dry concrete and asphalt.

WEIGHT:
Kerb weight 33.0 cwt (3,695 lb–1,675 kg) (with oil, water and half full fuel tank.) Distribution, per cent F, 50.7; R. 49.3. Laden as tested: 37 cwt (4,105 lb–1,865 kg).

TURNING CIRCLES:
Between kerbs L. 39ft 6in.; R, 34ft 11in. Between walls L. 41ft, 1in.; R 36ft 9in. steering wheel turns, lock to lock 3.5.

Standing ¼-mile
15.0 sec 92 mph
Standing kilometre
27.7 sec 116 mph
Test distance 1,005 miles
Mileage recorder 7 per cent over-reading

GEARING (with 185-15in. tyres)
Top . . . . 26.4 mph per 1,000 rpm
Inter. . . . . 18.7 mph per 1,000 rpm
Low . . . . 10.8 mph per 1,000 rpm

A brand new engine ready for installation in an Interceptor.

A new convertible bodyshell in the paint shop for undercoating.

Interceptors in varying stages of the painting process.

clean air combustion package), a redesign of the front suspension, refinements to the gearbox and improvements in the tyre equipment (with a revised axle ratio to suit different rolling radii). Power steering has been added to the standard specification, ventilation and demisting are improved and the headlamps have quartz-halogen bulbs.

Even before one opens a door there are obvious signs of better quality compared with the early cars. Working from panels shaped in Italy, Jensen reform the rough flanges, weld up and fill to make a body which as well as being elegant is free from blemish and ripple long before it enters the paint spray booth. Inside there is an extremely high class of finish, with a luxurious smell of real Connolly hide and satisfying fits to the complex trim around the instruments and fascia.

Like all Americans, the engine starts easily and idles smoothly at only 500rpm, with a sporty burble to its exhaust. At the peak of 4,600rpm it now develops 330bhp compared with 325 previously and although the torque is still quoted as 425 at 2,800rpm, the shape of the curve is a lot flatter.

With a power output like this in a car weighing 33cwt unladen, the results of pressing the accelerator are pretty electrifying to say the least. From rest 60mph is reached in only 6.4 sec and 100mph comes up in 18.2sec. Compared with our earlier test car, the latest one is slightly quicker, but only to the extent of less than 2sec all the way to 120mph. This was one of the rare cars which could reach 130mph from rest comfortably within the mile length of the MIRA horizontal straights. Even on a dreadfully wet day, when we had eventually

CONSUMPTION

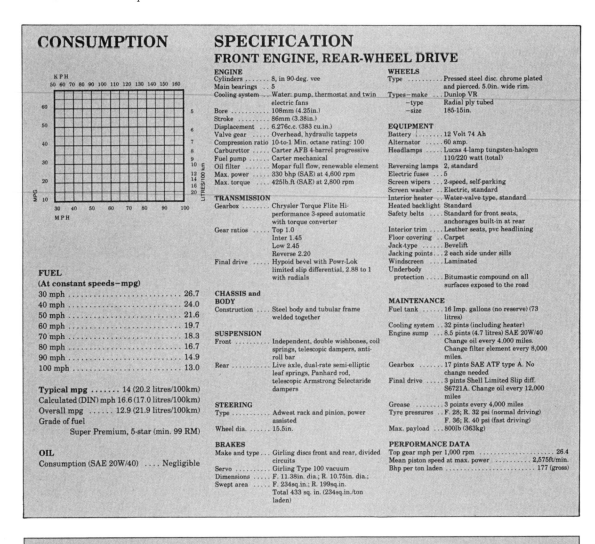

FUEL

(At constant speeds—mpg)

30 mph	26.7
40 mph	24.0
50 mph	21.6
60 mph	19.7
70 mph	18.3
80 mph	16.7
90 mph	14.9
100 mph	13.0

Typical mpg 14 (20.2 litres/100km)
Calculated (DIN) mph 16.6 (17.0 litres/100km)
Overall mpg 12.9 (21.9 litres/100km)
Grade of fuel
    Super Premium, 5-star (min. 99 RM)

OIL

Consumption (SAE 20W/40) .... Negligible

SPECIFICATION
FRONT ENGINE, REAR-WHEEL DRIVE

ENGINE
Cylinders .... 8, in 90-deg. vee
Main bearings .. 5
Cooling system ... Water: pump, thermostat and twin
    electric fans
Bore 108mm (4.25in.)
Stroke 86mm (3.38in.)
Displacement ... 6.276c.c. (383 cu.in.)
Valve gear ..... Overhead, hydraulic tappets
Compression ratio 10-to-1 Min. octane rating: 100
Carburettor ..... Carter AFB 4-barrel progressive
Fuel pump ...... Carter mechanical
Oil filter .... Mopar full flow, renewable element
Max. power ..... 330 bhp (SAE) at 4,600 rpm
Max. torque ..... 425lb.ft (SAE) at 2,800 rpm

TRANSMISSION
Gearbox .... Chrysler Torque Flite Hi-
    performance 3-speed automatic
    with torque converter
Gear ratios .... Top 1.0
    Inter 1.45
    Low 2.45
    Reverse 2.20
Final drive ..... Hypoid bevel with Powr-Lok
    limited slip differential, 2.88 to 1
    with radials

CHASSIS and BODY
Construction .... Steel body and tubular frame
    welded together

SUSPENSION
Front .... Independent, double wishbones, coil
    springs, telescopic dampers, anti-
    roll bar
Rear .... Live axle, dual-rate semi-elliptic
    leaf springs, Panhard rod,
    telescopic Armstrong Selectaride
    dampers

STEERING
Type .... Adwest rack and pinion, power
    assisted
Wheel dia. ...... 15.5in.

BRAKES
Make and type ... Girling discs front and rear, divided
    circuits
Servo .... Girling Type 100 vacuum
Dimensions ..... F. 11.38in. dia.; R. 10.75in. dia.;
Swept area ..... F. 234sq.in.; R. 199sq.in.
    Total 433 sq. in. (234sq.in./ton
    laden)

WHEELS
Type .... Pressed steel disc. chrome plated
    and pierced. 5.0in. wide rim.
Types—make .. Dunlop VR
   −type   Radial ply tubed
   −size   185-15in.

EQUIPMENT
Battery .... 12 Volt 74 Ah
Alternator ..... 60 amp.
Headlamps ..... Lucas 4-lamp tungsten-halogen
    110/220 watt (total)
Reversing lamps 2, standard
Electric fuses ... 5
Screen wipers ... 2-speed, self-parking
Screen washer .. Electric, standard
Interior heater .. Water-valve type, standard
Heated backlight Standard
Safety belts .... Standard for front seats,
    anchorages built-in at rear
Interior trim .... Leather seats, pvc headlining
Floor covering .. Carpet
Jack-type ...... Bevelift
Jacking points ... 2 each side under sills
Windscreen .... Laminated
Underbody
  protection ..... Bitumastic compound on all
    surfaces exposed to the road

MAINTENANCE
Fuel tank ...... 16 Imp. gallons (no reserve) (73
    litres)
Cooling system .. 32 pints (including heater)
Engine sump ... 8.5 pints (4.7 litres) SAE 20W/40
    Change oil every 4,000 miles.
    Change filter element every 8,000
    miles.
Gearbox .... 17 pints SAE ATF type A. No
    change needed
Final drive ..... 3 pints Shell Limited Slip diff.
    S6721A. Change oil every 12,000
    miles
Grease .... 3 points every 4,000 miles
Tyre pressures .. F. 28; R. 32 psi (normal driving)
    F. 36; R. 40 psi (fast driving)
Max. payload ... 800lb (363kg)

PERFORMANCE DATA
Top gear mph per 1,000 rpm 26.4
Mean piston speed at max. power .... 2,575ft/min.
Bhp per ton laden .... 177 (gross)

1	Bonnet assy − unpainted − plain/louvred		top		− front wheel RH	25	Front wing assy RH
2	Pillar assy RH/LH − door − front	9	Support − front rail hinge area RH	18	Front stoneguard − front wheel LH	26	Front wing assy LH
3	Box assy RH − air collection	10	Support − front rail hinge area LH	19	Sealing rubber − stoneguard	27	Front panel assy
4	Box assy LH − air collection	11	Mtg. assy − rear stoneguard RH	20	Bracket − outer RH − stoneguard − front	28	Plinth assy − side light RH
5	Air duct and inner wheelarch assy RH	12	Mtg. assy − rear stoneguard LH	21	Bracket − outer LH − stoneguard − front	29	Plinth assy − side light LH
6	Air duct and inner wheelarch assy LH	13	Rear stoneguard − front wheel RH	22	Bracket − inner RH − stoneguard − front	30	Front crossmember assy
7	Extension panel RH − wheelarch − top	14	Rear stoneguard − front wheel LH	23	Bracket − inner LH − stoneguard − front	31	Valance − front RH
8	Extension panel LH − wheelarch −	15	Extension panel RH − wheelarch − front	24	Extension assy − front	32	Valance − front LH
		16	Extension panel LH − wheelarch − front			33	Joint piece − centre − valance
		17	Front stoneguard			34	Piping − valance to panel
						35	Side member assy RH
						36	Side member assy LH

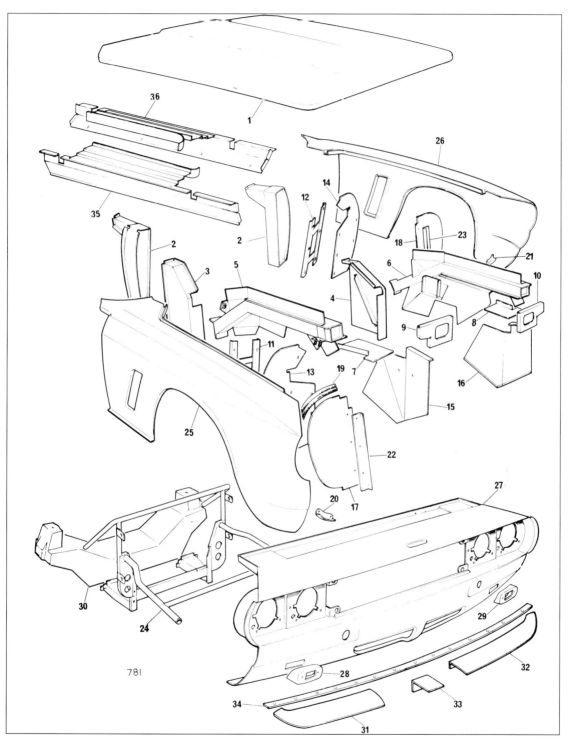

This complex jigsaw of metal shapes gives an idea of the make-up and
construction of the Interceptor panels and fittings. The inner plates are cut by
hand and welded to the chassis, whilst the outer pressings are stamped out;
gaps are lead-filled after fitting.

1	Reservoir assy – fluid	24	Lever – pedal c/w bushes	42	Clip – hose to manifold	58	Washer – spring
2	Label – fluid level	25	Bush – pedal lever	43	Adaptor – non-return valve	59	Nut
3	Cap – reservoir	26	Bolt – pivot – pedal	44	Spacer – adaptor	60	Disc – brake – front
4	Switch – fluid warning light	27	Washer – plain – pivot – pedal	45	Gasket – spacer – adaptor	61	Pipe – 3-way to hose RH
5	Hose – inlet pipe	28	Nut – lock	46	Adaptor – vacuum manifold	62	Pipe clamp – triple
6	Clip – hose	29	Plate – pedal pad	47	Connector assy – vacuum control	63	Connector – 3-way
7	Pipe – inlet – rear brakes	30	Bolt – plate to pedal lever	48	Connector – vacuum control	64	Bolt – connector to crossmember
8	Pipe – inlet – front brakes	31	Pedal pad – rubber	49	Tubing – vacuum control	65	Pipe – 3-way to hose
9	Clip – fluid reservoir	32	Connection – 'T'	50	Hose – 'T' connection/non-return valve	66	Pipe clamp – single
10	Bracket – mounting – fluid reservoir	33	Hose – vacuum 'T'/air condition-ing 'T'	51	Hose – inline non-return valve/'T' connection	67	Washer – shakeproof – HP hose
11	Screw	34	Restrictor – hose	52	Connector – double end	68	Nut – lock – HP hose
12	Washer – plain – large	35	Non-return valve – inline	53	Pipe – M/C to 3-way connector	69	Hose – high pressure – front
13	Washer – plain	36	Clip – hose – non-return valve	54	Pipe – M/C to double-end connection	70	Pipe – hose to caliper RH/LH
14	Washer – spring	37	Connection 'T' – air conditioning	55	Pipe clamp – double	71	Spring – return – brake pedal
15	Nut	38	Hose – 'T' connection to chassis connection	56	Screw – pipe to wheelarch	72	Bracket – stop-light switch
16	Servo less master cylinder	39	Clip – hose – 'T' and chassis connection	57	Washer – plain	73	Swtich – stop light
17	Kit – non-return valve – servo	40	Vacuum connection – chassis	58	Washer – spring	74	End stop – switch
18	Master cylinder	41	Hose – 'T' connection to inlet manifold			75	Nut – lock – switch
19	Washer – spring					76	Box – brake pedal
20	Nut					77	Gasket – sealing – pedal box
21	Pin – clevis – servo to pedal lever						
22	Washer – plain						
23	Pin – split						

gear mph per 1,000rpm goes up a little from 25.6 to 26.4.

During acceleration runs we found that the hydraulic valve gear did not 'pump up' at 5,100rpm as on the earlier car, and 5,500rpm was possible and usable. There is a red sector on the rev counter from 5,100 to deter the use of high revs and most of the time there is an abundance of torque much lower down the rev band. But it made quite a difference on top and this time we recorded 137mph in two directions with the rev counter reading 5,400rpm.

The latest Torque flite transmission has a cushion clutch to reduce the snatch when changing up or down and it is a real example of how smooth an automatic box can be. There is hardly a pause in the steady accelerative pull during upshifts, and the kickdown quality is particularly good. The selector has a big round knob, well placed and easy to

hold, with a push-button in the top to unlock it. Holding the lower gears with the over-ride we ran to 95 and 55mph at 5,100rpm.

Girling now make the brakes instead of Dunlop and sizes are altered slightly. With discs front and rear there is no fade what-so-ever and the response is much lighter than before. It now takes only 60lb effort to get a maximum (0.98) g stop, about half the previous figure. There is always a very reassuring bite to the pedal.

Our previous criticisms of the steering have been heeded, and a power-assisted system is now fitted. It is a special installation by Adwest, with a servo rack and pinion and a steering oil cooler up front. The big (17in dia.) wood-rimmed steering wheel has been replaced with a 15½in leather one with the same number of turns (3½) between rather cumbersome and uneven turning circles of 41ft left, 37ft right, between kerbs.

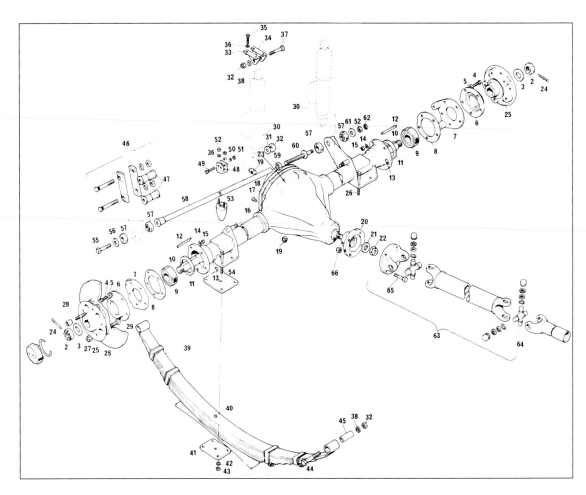

The Interceptor had an open prop-shaft, linked to a hypoid rear axle which incorporated a 'PowrLok' limited slip differential. Final drive ratio was 3.07:1. Suspension was by semi-elliptic dual-rate leaf springs with rubber button inter-leaf spacers. It also used Armstrong telescopic dampers and a Panhard rod.

All the work has now gone out of parking but there is a dead patch around the straight ahead position which leads to slight instability at speed. Turning the wheel a few degrees in this region made the car deflect all right, but it stayed on the chosen rate of turn without pulling straight on its own. This kind of behaviour is often caused by too much friction in the steering swivels rather than insufficient castor. To improve the whole front end and give adjustments not previously provided for, the front suspension is now by means of Alford and Alder ball-jointed wishbones with telescopic dampers, instead of by lower wishbones and upper lever-arm dampers with bushed king-pins.

One of the benefits claimed is better front end damping. Our car had covered almost 12,000 miles by the time we had completed our test and the dampers at the front were too weak. In relation to those at the rear they were out of balance, causing the car to float and pitch at the front about the rear end as a pivot. This spoilt what would otherwise be a very good ride. Armstrong Select-a-ride rear dampers are fitted and experiments with their four settings altered only the fierceness of the disturbances without reducing the discomfort.

1	Axle assy – rear	21	Washer – yoke to carrier		absorber to bracket	53	Bump rubber
2	Nut – hub	22	Nut – yoke to carrier	38	Washer – plain	54	Bolt – spring to axle
3	Washer – hub nut	23	Differential PowrLok assy	39	Spring – road – rear	55	Bolt – panhard rod
4	Bolt	24	Pin – split – hub nut	40	Bolt – toe	56	Washer – plain – panhard rod
5	Washer – plain	25	Hub assy – rear	41	Plate – bottom – spring	57	Bush – rubber – panhard rod
6	Retainer – hub – oil seal	26	Disc brake – rear	42	Washer – plain – spring to axle	58	Tube – panhard rod assy
7	Plate – adaptor – rear LH	27	Nut – lock – disc to hub	43	Nut – lock – spring to axle	59	Nut – lock – spigot – panhard rod
8	Plate – adaptor – rear RH	28	Nut – wheel	44	Bolt – spring to chassis	60	Screwed spigot assy
9	Shim bearing – hub	29	Bolt – disc to hub	45	Bush – road spring	61	Washer – plain – spigot
10	Shaft – axle	30	Shock absorber – rear	46	Shackle assy – rear	62	Nut – lock – spigot
11	Seal – oil	31	Washer – 'D' – shock absorber to axle	47	Bush – shackle	63	Propshaft assy
12	Key – axle shaft	32	Nut – lock	48	Bracket – bump rubber	64	Universal joint – propshaft
13	Nipple – grease	33	Bracket – outer – shock absorber	49	Bolt – bracket to chassis	65	Bolt – propshaft to axle
14	Washer – spring	34	Bracket – inner – shock absorber	50	Washer – spring – bracket to chassis	66	Nut – lock – propshaft to axle
15	Nut – nyloc	35	Screw – bracket to chassis	51	Nut		
16	Screw – cover to gear carrier	36	Washer – spring	52	Nut – bump rubber		
17	Cover – gear carrier	37	Bolt – shock				
18	Gasket – gear carrier cover						
19	Plug – drain and filler						
20	Yoke – pinion						

The relative rear end stiffness, especially in roll, caused us serious concern about the ultimate handling. Up to a very high cornering speed there was predictable understeer, but beyond what we found to be a very critical and sudden limit the back end would break away regardless of the amount of power being applied to the rear wheels. To put this criticism in perspective we should qualify it by saying that one expects a car of this calibre and price to have unusual roadholding powers at least the match for its considerable power.

We should also add that only an idiot is ever likely to encounter this limit on public roads under normal driving. It is the behaviour in an emergency which worries us, because once adhesion has been lost, recovery takes too long and when correction does take effect it is with a sudden whip which is very hard to catch.

If the going is slippery or one wants to make good time, the best way in this Jensen is to adopt the slow-in, fast-out technique in corners and to treat it as a point-and-squirt

machine. With all that torque on tap and such excellent brakes willing to take any punishment, there are no problems in getting along very fast indeed. When required, the selector can be flicked back a notch to give engine braking, and the eager beat of the dual exhausts is somehow indicative of unleashed power.

Even when pressing on at a lesser rate, the seats seem to be too slippery and rather lacking in lateral support. They are comfortable and well shaped for sitting on, but not for holding one in place. The smaller steering wheel is much more manageable, and its leather rim is nicer to touch.

Instrument and switch layout is unchanged but the rear fan demister have been replaced by a Triplex Hotline heated element in the glass. It is confined to the area seen in the mirror, which is small, but it works well. There is a measure of through-flow air, but not nearly enough to counter the considerable heat of the big vee-8 in our recent spell of hot weather. Face-level fresh-air ducts definitely do not pass enough volume and the air picks

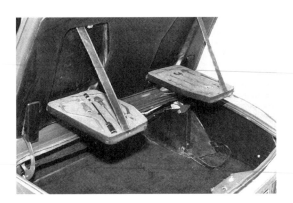

Jensen thoughtfully provided a decent set of basic tools, which were located in a pair of trays which could be dropped down when the flat boot-lid was opened.

Interceptor wipers generally gave good spread of clearance across the windscreen.

up heat on the way through. Separate fans boost the independent systems, but these are noisy. Temperature control for the heater is by a crude water valve with poor sensitivity.

Flick switches on the wood veneered central console are identified by symbols and there is a double scale temperature gauge right under the driver's eyes between the matching rev counter and speedometer.

There is a limited amount of room in the back for two more people, but this is a 2 + 2 rather than a four-seater. Getting into the rear compartment is a game only for children and those with supple muscles and small feet.

One of the most enjoyable extras fitted on the test car was a Voxson radio and stereo tape player with four speakers. Tape cassettes are slotted-in where tuning push-buttons normally fill the face, so radio stations must be found by hand. The extra dimension of stereo in a car like this adds tremendously to the pleasures of driving it.

Noise levels on the whole are low and it is barely necessary to raise one's voice or the volume of the radio when cruising at 70 mph or 100 mph for that matter. Overall the exhaust seemed louder than we remembered on other Jensens and road noise seemed less. The quartz-halogen bulbs in the four head-

lamp system add a lot of brilliance, especially on main beams when there is a white blaze of light scorching its way through the night.

Overall the Interceptor is a very refined car, with tremendous performance and a high standard of finish. It is more for the successful tycoon than sporty playboy, and treated with the respect such a powerful machine deserves it is an invigorating way to get about. All it lacks at the moment is better ultimate handling and a more sophisticated heating and ventilation system.

LAUNCH OF THE MARK III

The Mark III Interceptor was introduced at Earls Court in 1971, and came into being because it incorporated some of the flagship's features, rather than because the Mark II had been updated. The face-lift was confined to the repositioning of the front number-plate, now placed below the revised front bumper. At the back, there was now a single light to illuminate the number-plate and, again, the bumper was altered slightly. The vents on the front wings now incorporated side indicators, and headlights were set in black-painted cast-alloy surrounds.

Like most cars with twin headlight arrangements, the Interceptor's provided excellent illumination on main beam, but the cut-off when switching to dip was a bit abrupt. Modern quartz-halogen lamps are an improvement.

The Mark III Interceptor was launched alongside the SP and short-lived FF III at Earls Court in 1971. The new GKN alloy wheels substantially improved the image, and the cars now took on a raised nose posture in deference to US headlight height regulations.

Jensen publicity shot of the Mark III interior, showing eight-track stereo radio and padded steering wheel. All Interceptors apart from a few Mark Is used automatic transmission, and this car has the latest shift lever.

A well-used Mark III interior, showing how the auxiliary dials are all angled towards the driver. The owner has substituted a leather-rim wheel for the standard one.

Powerhouse of the Mark III. Chrysler engine specification changed almost yearly, so Jensen Motors took whatever was in current production. Prominent in the engine bay, just ahead of the pancake air filter, is the air-conditioning pump.

Inside the car, the front seats were modified to give better support, and the comforts of those in the rear were catered for by fitting a central armrest. The trim design called for large, unbroken spaces of leather with no tucks or seams visible, to the extent that no fewer than seven hides were used to trim each vehicle. The air-conditioning system was improved and, although still listed as an option, it was fitted in the majority of cars. Central locking became standard, and the ignition switch was illuminated for some fifteen seconds after the driver entered the car so that he could find it in the dark.

If you bought an early Mark III car, you might have got the G-Series 6.3-litre engine with Carter carburettor; if you bought a later model from 1972 it would have the H-Series 7.2-litre lump with its Holley carb. This was a reflection on what Chrysler themselves were doing with their engines because, basically, Jensen had to take what they were given. Emission regulations threatened to emasculate the sizeable power output of the

big engine and, by 1973, it was down from 330bhp to 300bhp.

The major oil crisis of 1973 was not yet upon us, and there was still room at the top of the motoring world for vehicles whose owners were virtual strangers to frugality. So it was that Jensen took the 400cu in Chrysler 7,212cc unit and placed it in a Mark II Interceptor. This high-compression engine was fed by three twin-choke Holley carburettors and produced a massive 330bhp, when the basic 6.3-litre engine was already good for 284bhp. The carburettor set-up provided the inspiration for the naming of the new flagship; it was to be the SP, or Six-Pack, which today sounds like a consignment of canned beer but in 1971 implied a cluster of Holley carburettor chokes.

This apparatus was, if anything, the SP's Achilles' heel, for it required tuning roughly once a month. And the SP was also the hot one, literally, and in order to cope with the extra under-bonnet heat, was given four rows of louvres running along the length of the bonnet. US headlight-level regulations

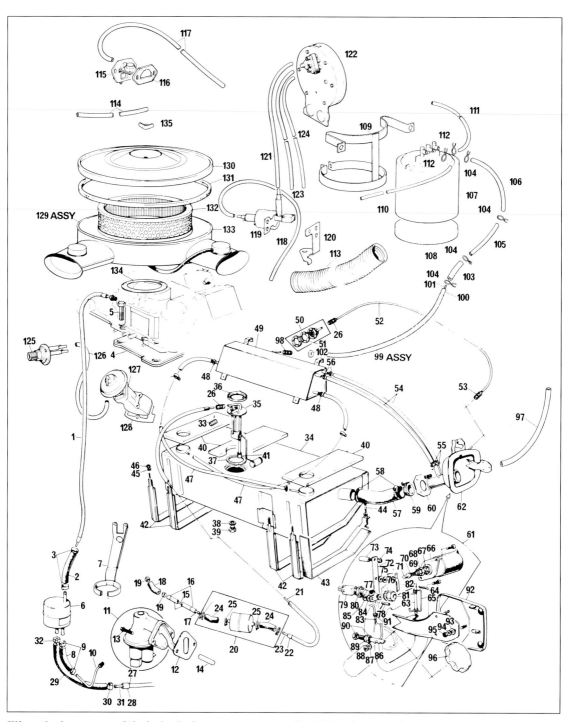

When the bonnet was lifted, the fuel system was virtually hidden beneath the mighty pancake air filter. The system was worked by a mechanical pump, incorporating a filter in the fuel line. Early models used a Carter carburettor; the 7.2-litre cars were fitted with 4-barrel Holley carbs, reverting to Carter with the Mark III and J-Series cars. The exception was the SP which used three twin-choke Holleys to attain its towering 330bhp.

1 Pipe assy – carburettor to vapour separator
2 Connector hose – carburettor to vapour separator
3 Clip – pipe
4 Gasket – carburettor to manifold
5 Bolt – carburettor to manifold
6 Vapour separator
7 Bracket assy – vapour separator
8 Connector hose – vapour separator to fuel pump
9 Clip
10 Pipe assy – vapour separator to pump
11 Fuel pump
12 Gasket – fuel pump
13 Screw – fuel pump fixing
14 Push rod – fuel pump
15 Pipe assy – pump to filter
16 End sleeve – pipe
17 Tube – connector
18 Connector – pipe to pump
19 Clip – pipe to pump connector
20 Fuel filter
21 Pipe assy – filter to fuel tank
22 End sleeve – pipe
23 Tube – connector
24 Connector – filter to pipes
25 Clip – filter to pipe connectors
26 Reducing connector – pipe to fuel tank
27 Return pipe – separator to tank
28 End sleeve – pipe
29 Connector tube – return pipe to separator
30 Clip – connector tube
31 Connector tube – return pipe to connector tube
32 Clip – connector tube
33 Reducing connector – return pipe to tank

34 Fuel tank less float unit
35 Float unit – fuel tank
36 Locking ring – float unit
37 Sealing ring – float unit
38 Gasket – drain plug – fuel tank
39 Drain plug – fuel tank
40 Felt pad – fuel tank
41 Filter (nylon mesh) – fuel tank
42 Strap assy – fuel tank
43 Strip – rubber – fuel tank strap
44 Bolt – tank strap to chassis
45 Washer – plain
46 Nut – lock
47 Pipe – expansion tank to fuel tank
48 Clip – expansion tank/fuel tank pipe
49 Expansion tank
50 Relief valve – expansion tank
51 Gasket – relief valve
52 Pipe – expansion tank to filler bowl
53 Reducing connector – expansion tank to bowl pipe
54 Pipe – expansion tank to filler neck
55 Clip – expansion tank/filler neck pipe
56 Clip – expansion tank/filler neck pipe
57 Hose – fuel tank to filler neck
58 Clip – tank to filler neck hose
59 Grommet – filler neck
60 Sealing plate – filler neck
61 Fillter bowl assy comp (less lid)
62 Filler bowl assy
63 Hinge pin
64 Split pin
65 Spring – hinge
66 Solenoid
67 Locknut – solenoid
68 Adaptor screw –

solenoid
69 Locknut – solenoid to rod
70 Spring – return solenoid
71 Rod – solenoid
72 Operating lever – solenoid
73 Boss – lever
74 Locknut – boss to lever
75 Washer – nylon – solenoid to bowl
76 Push on fix – solenoid to bowl
77 Washer – nylon – lever to bowl
78 Pin – spirol – lever to bowl
79 Switch – warning light
80 Locknut – switch to bowl
81 End stop – switch
82 Actuator spring
83 Link – rod – lid latch
84 Washer – nylon – link to lever
85 Push on fix – link to lever
86 Latch
87 Washer – nylon – link to latch
88 Push on fix – link to latch
89 Washer – fibre – latch to bowl
90 Locknut – latch to bowl
91 Grommet – filler bowl
92 Lid – filler bowl
93 Washer – plain – door to hinge
94 Washer – spring
95 Nut
96 Filler cap – fuel
97 Overflow tube – filler bowl
98 Reducing connector – expansion tank to hose connector pipe
99 Pipe assy – expansion tank to hose connector
100 End sleeve – pipe
101 Tube – connector
102 Grommet
103 Hose – connector
104 Hose clip

105 Pipe – hose connector to hose
106 Hose – pipe to carbon canister
107 Carbon canister assy
108 Filter – carbon canister
109 Mounting bracket – carbon canister
110 Hose – canister to carburettor
111 Hose – canister to carburettor bowl
112 Clip – hose
113 Cover – hose
114 Hose – carburettor to OSAC valve
115 OSAC valve assy
116 Seal
117 Hose – OSAC valve to distributor
118 Hose – carburettor to EGR solenoid
119 EGR solenoid
120 Bracket EGR solenoid
121 Hose – EGR solenoid to vacuum amplifier
122 Vacuum amplifier
123 Hose – vacuum amplifier to vacuum take off
124 Hose – vacuum amplifier to thermostatic control unit
125 Thermostatic control unit
126 Hose – thermostatic control unit to EGR valve
127 EGR valve
128 Gasket – EGR valve flange
129 Air cleaner assy
130 Cover – air cleaner
131 Gasket – cover to body
132 Element
133 Body – air cleaner
134 Gasket – air cleaner to carburettor

The SP was introduced in October 1971 to replace the costly FF as Jensen's company flagship. The 'SP' identification stood for Six-Pack, a reference to the three twin-choke Holley carburettors employed on the higher-compression 330bhp 7.2-litre Chrysler V8. Only 208 units were produced.

meant raising the front-ride height by almost 2in, so SPs and Mark III Interceptors always had that about-to-leap posture; generally speaking, altering ride-heights like this does the handling no favours.

The SP was introduced alongside the Mark III at the Earls Court Show in October 1971, together with the last of the FFs, and in order to keep abreast of contemporary trend in finishes, the SP was given that mixed blessing, the vinyl roof. This is fine when new, but soon looks tacky and, later on, tatty, as well as harbouring damp and its attendant evils. On the brighter side, seating and door trims were revised, as for the Mark III car, with central locking facility, air-conditioning and state-of-the-art hi-fi Lear-jet eight-track stereo fitted as standard in the SP. Best of all was the arrival of some decent wheels. The GKN five-spoke alloys meant Interceptors could also accommodate wider and more modern GR70 spec tyres.

The SP was not a great deal faster than its predecessor, the Mark II, mainly because it required five-star high octane petrol and did not really come into its own until it was doing 80mph (130kph), when it took only another six seconds to get to 100mph

Apart from a vinyl roof, the SP was also identifiable by its extensively louvred bonnet which assisted dissipation of heat from the engine bay. This was the first model to get the new GKN alloy wheels and a side indicator in the front wing air vent.

(160kph), a full second quicker than the 6.3-litre car. In normal driving, as opposed to just seeing how fast it would go, the SP would get to 110mph (170kph) using only one of the three Holleys. But a sudden application of the right foot would have the carbs sucking like mad for air, the Torqueflite winding itself up, and the engine note rumbling to a roar, and the beast would take off. Throttle-response was somewhat esoteric; due to their automatic linkage, the extra chokes would start to function as engine load increased, producing a surge of power with no extra pressure on the accelerator pedal.

This could all be very well when going up a hill, but back off the throttle and the power could die away suddenly or, alternatively, it could flood in when cornering loads placed more strain on the engine. As with virtually any automatic transmission, when acceleration from rest was desired, the SP in 'drive' mode would take a moment to gird up its loins, so to speak, but for a more immediate effect, the gears could be selected manually using 'hold'. The legacy of this kind of behaviour, assuming you weren't apprehended by the traffic police, was a fuel consumption of between 10 and 14mpg (355

The J-Series Interceptor; it doesn't seem such a large car when viewed from above.

Classic proportions of the 1974 J-Series Mark III.

The J-Series' power unit was the 7.2-litre Chrysler engine with single Carter Thermoquad carburettor.

(Left)   Huge 'greenhouse' rear window provides access to luggage space.

Chassis number prefix for the Interceptor series from 1974 onwards	
First digit describes *model type*	2 Interceptor
Second digit describes *body style*	2 Saloon, 3 Convertible
Third digit describes *drive*	1 LHD (US), 2 LHD (Europe), 3 LHD (Europe), 4 RHD
Fourth digit describes *market area*	0 US, Austria, Switzerland and UK
	1 Germany and Australia
	2 France and Japan
	3 Belgium, Holland and New Zealand
	4 Hong Kong

and 495km/100l). The SP and the Mark III cars were endowed with a new dual-circuit braking system with 10.7in (270mm) discs for hauling it down from these excesses. There was now no brake-fade which had beset some earlier models.

The SP production run lasted only two years. Chrysler had been at loggerheads with the exhaust-emissions regulations starting to take off the in the US, and the Six-Pack engine just could not comply. When they dropped it, obviously Jensen had to as well. In its place, the Mark III was kitted out with all the SP's extras, even down to the 7.2-litre engine, still in 330bhp trim with Carter Thermoquad carburettor, and called the J-Series Interceptor.

It is the view of Development Engineer John Page that the Mark II Interceptor with the 383cu in engine was the best; he believes it was a far better engine than the 440 7.2-litre lump. Further, the Mark II was faster than the Mark III but, not surprisingly, it wouldn't beat the SP. But then the SP was relatively unreliable, as the carburettors needed to be tuned every month. The SP is one of those cars which bears the epitaph, 'When it was on song, it was a great car'. Jensen had a great deal of trouble with the carburettors, and a lot of them were converted back to the single four-barrel Carter carb because owners couldn't cope with having to retune the carburettors every 300 miles (480km) or so. It seems that Holley carburettors have never been a success on the car.

Because of their construction and the thickness of metal used to build them, Inter-ceptors in general have suffered from heat build-up under the bonnet, which in an American car with a similar engine is less acute because it has a bigger engine bay. The Interceptor's engine is shrouded and squashed in, and even the louvres didn't alleviate the problem.

CHASSIS NUMBERING

After the J-Series Interceptors, the company reworked the chassis numbering system, which had until then followed on in the manner of the 541. From 1974, the cars were known as S4-Interceptors, and are not to be taken for the Mark IV cars constructed after 1984; these later Interceptors are also known, confusingly, as Series Four cars, because it was felt they differed so little from the old Mark IIIs. The S4s of 1974 have a numbering system of which the first digit establishes the model, the second tells which body style it is, the third describes whether it is left- or right-hand drive, and the fourth defines the car's designated destination. So, for example, 2340 would be a right-hand-drive Interceptor Convertible sold in the UK.

In practice, the S4 cars displayed the J-badge just on the back panel, and this was the only means of recognizing the S4 from the later J-Series cars. Internally, the S4 was enhanced with the fitting of a walnut dash-board and similar trim panels on the centre console. The S4 also got the late-model US-spec steering wheel, which was a more up-to-date design.

John Page

Now aged forty-seven, John Page has worked at Jensen since 1968. At the time he recalls there was still an overlap with C-V8s and Interceptors. The outgoing models were being finished and there were about three Interceptors a week coming off the assembly line. John went straight into the service department as a mechanic, and worked there until 1970 when the present parts and service facility was set up. In early 1973, he went into the technical service side as part of a team of engineers in an administrational and trouble-shooting capacity. At the end of 1974 he returned to the shop-floor as foreman, where he remained until the closure in 1976. 'We were made redundant on the Friday night and started back on the Monday morning working for Jensen Parts and Service, under Bob Edmiston. In 1977, Edmiston took on the Subaru franchise, and I went over to Subaru tech until 1980, when he began importing Maseratis and de Tomasos, and I worked on those as a mechanic.'

'In 1982 I returned to Jensen, which by then was owned by Ian Orford, and I was employed as Development Engineer. Basically I initiate and develop all the new components and equipment we end up fitting on the cars.'

'I did a bit of travelling when I was in technical services. I went to see Harold Robbins on his yacht at Cannes. A couple of months earlier, he had been to the factory to collect his new Mark III Convertible and driven it back to the south of France, and then he asked for someone to fly out and do its first service and check it over. He also had a Mark I Interceptor which he asked me to look at while I was out there. He put me up in a hotel, and I had dinner aboard his yacht in the harbour one night, which was very nice.'

'I went to Madrid to sort out a couple of cars there, and in recent years, we've sold several Interceptors in Saudi, Oman and places like that. One time I had to go to Jeddah in Saudi Arabia, where a customer's car had been damaged in transit. It had been air-freighted out, but when it was landed and transported to his palace, the bonnet was found to be damaged. They had taken the bonnet off to repair it, but for some reason the air cleaner was missing and the carb had filled up with sand. I had to spend some time cleaning the carb and the fuel system out, changing the oil filters just to make sure that nothing had got inside it, then just tuned it up for him.'

'The desert is a poor environment to be running a car like that in, and generally they have a hard life. But back in the seventies a lot of the cars went out to Saudi and places, and now it's the sons of the fathers who are buying them. In between times you've had all the Mercs and all the limousines you can think of, but for some strange reason, the Interceptor appealed to the sons because they remember their father having one. They all seem to be princes, and one prince had his car done in exactly the same colour scheme as his father's car had been ten years earlier. They prefer the Saloon version with air-conditioning, because it's too hot with the roof down in a Convertible.'

There's no doubt in John Page's mind which was the best of the Interceptors: 'A Mark II Interceptor with the Carter AVS carb is a very nice car, and if I was going to buy one, that's what I'd get. The later ones are plusher inside, with the walnut dashboard, and so on, but I prefer the Mark II. But by and large they are owned by people who have a restricted classic car insurance policy and they are only brought out in summer, so we do very little servicing these days. People don't put any miles on them so it never comes due. When I'm stuck in a traffic jam on the M6 I think I'm glad I've only got a 1,600cc engine, instead of 5,000-odd chugging away. I've gone Green in my old age, but in the ideal world you'd have a little car to commute in and something that you fancy for the odd blast around.'

VARIATIONS ON THE THEME

There were two variations on the Interceptor theme: the Convertible was one, introduced in 1974, of which 467 were produced before the factory closure in 1976. It was always popular in the US, and Jensen remained one of the few manufacturers who were not fazed by the prospect of Federal regulations banning the import of rag-top cars; in the event, of course, this never happened.

Basically, the Convertible has the same chassis as the Saloon. Many regular production cars which are converted into cabriolets require considerable strengthen-

A 1975 Convertible shows off its clean lines.

Louvred bonnets made for improved cooling.

J-Series cars are identified by the logo on the C-pillar.

One option for J-Series owners, and especially US imports, was the sheepskin inserts in the seats' upholstery.

Newly-restored S4 Interceptor at the factory.

J-Series cars retained the plastic-covered fascia of earlier models, but a Philips radio-cassette player was fitted instead of the dated eight-track unit.

Launched in March 1974, the Convertible used the 7.2-litre Chrysler V8, which produced 330bhp and delivered effortless performance.

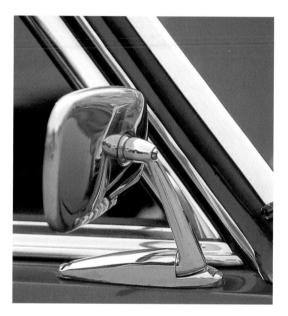

In the days when chrome plating ruled, J-Series cars could match door mirrors with the best of them.

The Convertible has a single air-vent with side indicator, plus GKN alloy wheels.

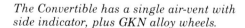

Front jacking point cover incorporated in the J-Series car's stainless-steel sill cover.

Rear-light cluster of the Mark III J-Series cars.

From 1971, Mark III and SP model Interceptors got the 6½in GKN alloy wheels, which proved a major stylistic improvement.

1	Manifold – intake	18	Bracket – heat shield		drive (matched pair)	53 Clamp – distributor mounting
2	Bolt – intake manifold	19	Heat shield – exhaust manifold – RH	35	Belt – fan and idler	54 Heater cowl – upper
3	Packing – silencer – tappet	20	Gasket – cylinder head cover	36	Pulley – water pump	55 Heater cowl – lower
4	Gasket – intake manifold	21	Bracket – accelerator cable	37	Pulley – crankshaft	56 Hose – connection – cowl to air cleaner
5	Reinforcement	22	Cylinder head	38	Damper – crankshaft vibration	57 Grommet – air cleaner
6	Bracket – HT lead	23	Gasket – cylinder head	39	Pulley – idler	58 Air cleaner – crank case vent inlet
7	Transmitter – oil pressure	24	Stud – manifold	40	Bracket – idler pulley fan belt	59 Hose – vent to carburettor
8	Adaptor – oil pressure switch	25	Manifold – exhaust RH/LH	41	Shield – idler pulley fan belt	60 Clip – hose
9	Oil pressure switch	26	Stick – oil level	42	Spacer – idler pulley bracket support	61 Base – oil filler cap
10	Cover – cylinder head – RH	27	Tube – oil level stick	43	Cover – chain case	62 Cap – oil filler
11	Bracket – support – HT lead – O/S – front	28	Connection – water outlet	44	Gasket – chain- case cover	63 Grommet – crankcase vent valve
12	Separator – ignition cable	29	Gasket – water outlet connection	45	Seal – oil – chain- case cover	64 Valve – vent
13	Support – HT lead – O/S – rear	30	Thermostat	46	Short engine assy	65 Valve – exhaust gas recirculation
14	Cover – cylinder head – LH	31	Transmitter – temperature	47	Dowel	66 Amplifier – vacuum
15	Support – HT lead – N/S – rear	32	Adaptor – transmitter	48	Strainer oil c/w pipe	67 Bracket – vacuum amplifier
16	Grommet – support – HT lead	33	Belt – p/s pump drive	49	Gasket – sump	68 Bracket – front
17	Separator – cable – front – N/S	34	Belt – pulley alternator; A/C and alternator	50 51 52	Sump – less drain plug Plug – drain Gasket – plug	69 Idler c/w bearing

ing underneath the bodyshell. But the Interceptor chassis needs only to have a couple of brackets welded on to the A-pillar which supports the windscreen frame, a plate welding between the rear wheelarches, and the sills beefed up a bit.

The roof was raised or lowered electrically by means of an hydraulic pump, but you couldn't do it on the run, so to speak, because it would only operate when the car was parked in neutral. The hydraulic pump worked two rams either side and ahead of the rear arches, which drew the hood back or pushed it forward; sustained pressure on the operating switch controlled the rear quarter-light windows.

The other latecomer in the Interceptor range was the Coupe, which was a Jensen concept, subcontracted to Panther, who are better known for vehicles such as the Kallista and the Solo. The concept was right, and the Convertible-style boot and XJ-6 rear window were successful, but the brown-tinted glass hoop was of questionable taste; like a lot of cars in the mid-1970s, the Coupe was lumbered with a vinyl roof. The Coupe badge came from the Marina parts bin; only fifty-four Coupes were built, for by October 1975, Jensen Motors was already in the hands of the receiver.

ENGINE DEVELOPMENT

Mechanically, the 6,276cc Chrysler V8 powerplant is a strong, reliable and un-stressed unit, which doesn't wear partic-ularly badly, and has no major shortcomings. The reputation for overheating was estab-lished early on, by the very cars presented to the automotive press at Goodwood in 1967, which is where the legend started. It is something which happens because of thermo-stat failure, or even the radiator silting up. The radiator's capacity was at best borderline, and the moment its capacity was compromised, it couldn't do its job. Weak electrical circuits sometimes failed to activate auxiliary cooling fans in traffic jams, with predictable results. These are only

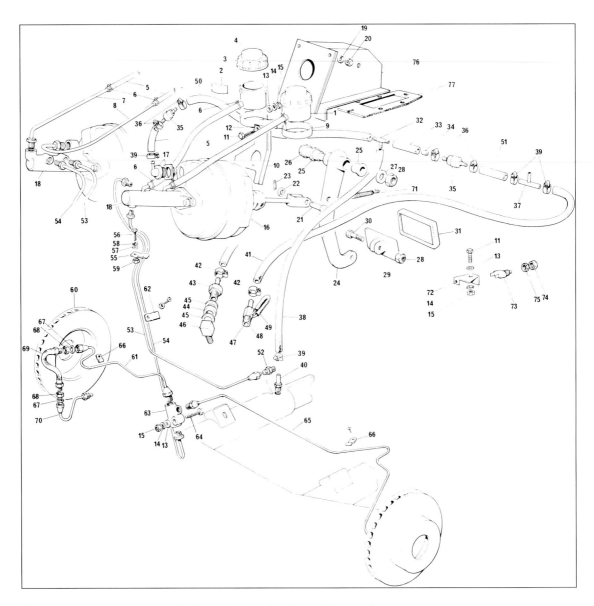

There was a separate system for front and rear brakes, with a tandem master cylinder and servo assistance. The front was a hydraulically operated, self adjusting set-up by Girling with ventilated discs. Later models had a pad-wear indicator.

to abandon our test measurements, the Interceptor (which has only two-wheel drive remember) shot to 100mph in only 19.4sec and with remarkably little wheel-spin.

Radial-ply tyres are now optional, Dunlop Sport being fitted. These are slightly smaller than the cross-ply RS5s which used to be obligatory, so the axle ratio is changed from 3.07 to 2.88 to 1 to compensate. In fact, top

The Chrysler V8 exploded, showing the main sections, including sump pan,
block, head, cam covers, manifolds and pulleys. This unit was constantly
being modified and, in effect, Jensen had to take whatever they were offered.
Capacities fluctuated from 6.3 litres to 7.2 litres, back down to 5.9 litres. The
cam-covers bear the Jensen logo, however.

The Coupe's distinctive top provided another variation on the Interceptor theme. It was a leaner, sportier looking car than the Saloon.

The Coupe badge looks fine on the Interceptor, but its antecedents were rather more humble in origin; Jensen raided the Morris Marina parts bin.

Coupe tops had three different configurations: the majority had a brown-tinted glass panel, which formed a hoop over the top of the vehicle; there were three steel-roof versions where the top was fully integrated with the body and colour-coded likewise; then there were a very few models like this one whose vinyl-covered roof was just like a fixed-head hard-top.

Using the same attractive rear body treatment as the Convertible, the Coupe's rear screen came from the Jaguar XJ-6.

Rather than style the Coupe within the factory, Jensen went to specialist coachwork and replica builders Panther Westwind, then run by Bob Jankel, to get a really striking design treatment for the Inteceptor Coupe. Panther was fashionable in the 1970s for creating replicas based on the pre-war SS Jaguar, Bugatti Royale and the post-war Ferrari 125S.

The Interceptor Coupe is one of the rarest Jensens, with production totalling a mere fifty-four cars before the shut-down in 1976.

Stepping up the Interceptor range from a Mark II, a Mark III J-Series car, to a Convertible.

The Convertible provides one of the best possible means of enjoying the countryside.

Vinyl roof covering was fashionable in 1971, but could lead to corrosion problems with moisture getting underneath.

The 1974 J-Series Interceptor quite at home in front of a Renaissance facade; the car would have to wait almost ten years for its own 'rebirth'.

The final model produced by Jensen Motors Limited before the factory closure, the Coupe was introduced at the Earls Court Show in October 1975.

This painted Convertible shell has already been fitted with its front
suspension; note the ventilated front brake discs.

partly design faults, for given ideal operating circumstances, the cars would not encounter sufficiently adverse conditions to show up the weaknesses. Cropredy Bridge Garage solve the problem on earlier cars by rewiring the fan, installing a different thermostat, and ensuring that the water pump is to the correct specification.

Otherwise, the only other trouble spots are with the ancillaries: the nylon-toothed timing gear, which was used to reduce engine noise, tends to be fragile, while starter motors stop functioning from time to time, and carburettor problems occur as a result of old age. Some of the linkage systems are a little bit primitive and work loose and struggle a bit; otherwise they are very reliable. There is no requirement for specialist mechanical knowledge to work on the cars.

Jensen fell foul of a run of faulty heat treatment on crankshafts in the 380cu in Chrysler engines, of which they were not notified by Chrysler. The effect was that the crank developed lots of end float and, if it went too far, it damaged all the bearings. Jensen went through a programme of fitting modified bearings and, in some cases, new crankshafts, which Chrysler paid for. There were problems with the wiring for the cooling fans, but these were designed in the late 1960s, and the wiring was up to spec for that time. Since then, and particularly when the 440 engines were introduced, the cars started suffering from overheating problems because the radiator couldn't cope with the extra power; the fans were working harder, fuses were blowing and, of course, the fans then packed up, leading to overheating.

But then by 1974, there were bigger

radiators and better fans, and the problem was solved. Nowadays with the Mark IV, there are circuit breakers and Bosch fans, and the arrangement is much more sophisticated. The Bosch fan draws 40 per cent more air than the Lucas unit fitted previously. At the time though, Lucas was the motor you used, and that was that. Before 1976, the experimental department played about with all these things, whereas nowadays they do it as and when they can. Other improvements came in 1974, when a bigger radiator was installed, which necessitated moving the front sub-frame forward and widening it slightly. This meant that the roll bar was in the way, so that was just dropped down underneath the sub-frame. The roll bar's aspect now had a sort of kink at either end, whereas the earlier ones were straight.

There had been more than a thousand alterations to the Interceptor's specification from the Vignale-produced cars. The most major change with the Mark IV, produced from the renaissance in 1983, was the adoption of a far more efficient 5.9-litre Chrysler unit, which had a management system, fuel injection, and already corresponded with Federal Emissions legislation. The frontal treatment of the car was also updated slightly by the addition of a discreet air-dam under the front valance. Interiors were much the same as the Mk III cars, except that the Recaro seats were now electrically adjustable. At first it was very slow going, taking some six months to complete one car, but things have gradually improved. There is something of an advantage here; because of the slow, ten-week production schedule, customers were able to specify virtually anything they wanted.

UPHOLSTERING THE INTERCEPTOR

Eric Ward is still trimming Interceptors today, having been at Jensen for some forty years. He has seen the company metamorphose through just about every crisis, having worked on 541s, C-V8s, the 1950s Interceptor and the Healey 3000. 'The highest production was 150 a week, and we made them at Carters Green. We were making the A40 Sports with the aluminium body, and then we started to make the Austin Healey.' He remembers speaking to the two Jensen brothers, but in those days, 'the management was not as close to the shop floor as it is now'. He continues:

Today they are saying we are a team, but in those days it was them and us. We were trying to get as much as we could, and they were trying to pay us as little as they had to. But the workers then were fairer than they are now. I can remember the time in the early 1960s when we refused to have a redundancy so we went on two days a week for twenty-six weeks. It was just barely an existence then. My wages were £8.6s.6d for the two days. We had redundancies because the Austin Healey was up and down in production all the time, and you're at the mercy of the firm that's hiring you.

He describes how the upholstery process works:

We are supplied with the seat frames and rubbers, and the covers are cut out. The most important thing is that the patterning must be right. We made all our own patterns; Denis Price made the originals, and he's nearly eighty now. When I came to Jensen aged twenty-one, he was in his early thirties and he taught me nearly everything. Denis was a very good trimmer and pattern maker. He even patterned the Austin Healey up. I worked with Denis quite a lot, and I worked in the experiment and development shop. We used to try different materials, and find out which was the hardest wearing. Of course, rexine wasn't fire-proof like materials are

Full leather interior enhanced the Mark II FF's luxurious character.

Mark II cars retained the 6.3-litre engine, and were given rocker covers cast in aluminium, featuring the company logo.

Trimmer Eric Ward has upholstered three generations of Jensens; here he works on a seat for a new Interceptor.

today, which causes us problems now since we can't get things which were produced in the seventies for restoration jobs. Now, the materials must be fire retardant. Our cars have always been leather, but the first ones that came from Vignale's in Italy were plastic. But Kevin Beattie wanted leather, and we've always used Connolly hide, though it's not necessarily better than some of the other hides. It's thicker, and more flexible, but Bridge of Weir are coming up with some nice hides. I've trimmed Mr Wainwright's car in that.

Seven hides does seem an awful lot of leather for each car, but that's what it takes. Most of our patterns are plain with no tucks, rolls or ruches, and we try not to get a lot of scars in. The biggest hide we can get is just

under 60 square feet, and they can be as small as 34 square feet. So it's hard to estimate. You buy hides in square feet, and

It takes seven hides to upholster an Interceptor; Mark II FF door trim illustrates why.

From 1965, the sumptuous C-V8 interior had leather and Wilton carpet
upholstery, a wood-veneer fascia, plus an improved heating and demisting
system, including a heated rear window.

the suppliers measure every single little bit, including a lot of scrap.

The main part of the hide is the shoulders and back. The belly is usually pretty rough. Some companies include the neck, where there are a lot of wrinkles, and where you get a lot of warble fly. You see pictures where birds are pecking on the beast's neck; well, they are pulling the maggot out, leaving a scar and holes in the hide. There are scars in the belly, because grass can be sharp, and naturally, animals are injected. The reason we use so many hides is because we use the top quality, the first cut, so that's got all the scars on it anyway; the other hide cuts are rolled.

Furniture hide is thinner, but cars are now having thinner hides because people like ruches and pleats. I don't like that, because those high spots are going to wear out first. The company buys hides at around £150 a piece, so that's over a £1,000 without VAT for seven hides, before any manufacturing. So you can understand people charging a lot of money for retrims.

How much carpet do you think you'd need for an Interceptor? It's 40ft of carpet; 3.3ft wide, and 17.5ft long. That means playing your patterns perfectly. The carpet is 80 per cent wool, 20 per cent nylon, and it's Wilton, which is very expensive. That doesn't include the boot either. We have a lot of scrap hide, because we won't put it in the car unless it's good. Underneath the belly is no good really, but you can use that part of hide for piping or something like that.

Personally I prefer cloth, your backside doesn't slide around and it's warm in winter and doesn't burn you in summer. The trouble with hide is that if you scratch it, it can be faked up, but it's never really the same again. We try Connollizing them, but I usually advise a retrim. We can dye them, but underneath the hide, sweat has got in, the sun has dried out all the natural oils, and they are brittle. I say forget it, wait till you can afford to get it done right. I think it costs around £3,500 for a retrim.

In the very first Interceptor, the one which looked like the A40 convertible, our seats were made with blow-up rubbers in the back, so that you could blow them up and let them down to what you wanted. Dick Jensen was a devil, because he always used to try the seats, and he'd say we need a bit extra there. He had a bad back, so he was more sensitive than most people. Even in these modern Interceptor seats, they designed them so you could pull the cover down and put some more padding in the back. That's the kind of thing they used to think of. We had to make the rubbers then. We had to have the spring casings made, and then put rubber over them, and then hessian, to make them comfortable. Jensen could never afford to have a mould then in 1970–75. We are only just having moulds made now. Nobody uses Dunlopillo today though; the foam works better and is more resilient. I still like Dunlopillo to sit on, because it feels softer, but with these new foams there's no chance of a seat-frame working through because they are quite solid.

Because the bodies are hand-built, there are slight variations in each one and the trimmer has to measure up exactly every time. Also, virtually every car produced now has an order for different colour interiors. When we were in the old factory, there were lots of different people on different jobs. They had slipmen like me who moved around wherever they were needed. Sometimes they used to call up on the track 'that one's a little baggy there' and we'd have to alter it.

With the Mark IV, the upholstery also received the updating treatment. In fact, the seat design was completely new, and a decent amount of much-needed lateral support was built into the squab and seat back. Headrests with removable cord-covered pads were standard equipment. You moved the pad up or down according to your head height. The front-seat passenger was accorded stowage space with an extra glove compartment, and the rear-seat passengers were to do better too, given a deeper recess into which to sink.

Now Eric's considering working part-time after he retires, which is only four years away. He is fairly confident of finding work, recalling a part-time job he did some years ago for someone up north. It was an old Morris 8, and it was the worst job he has ever had to tackle. He has a 541 of his own, currently being restored, not at the factory, but by a chap who advertises in the *Jensen Owners' Club Magazine*.

FUTURE POWERPLANTS

The Hemi engine was Ian Orford's notion of making the Mark IV Interceptor into a very special car indeed. But so far, they have only fitted one Hemi engine, and that's the one in Hugh Wainwright's car. 'Hemi' refers to the shape of the hemispherical combustion chambers. Chrysler built a 426cu in Hemi in cast iron, a very powerful engine indeed, but today an American company casts the Hemi cylinder head in aluminium, and has modified the cylinder head so that you can

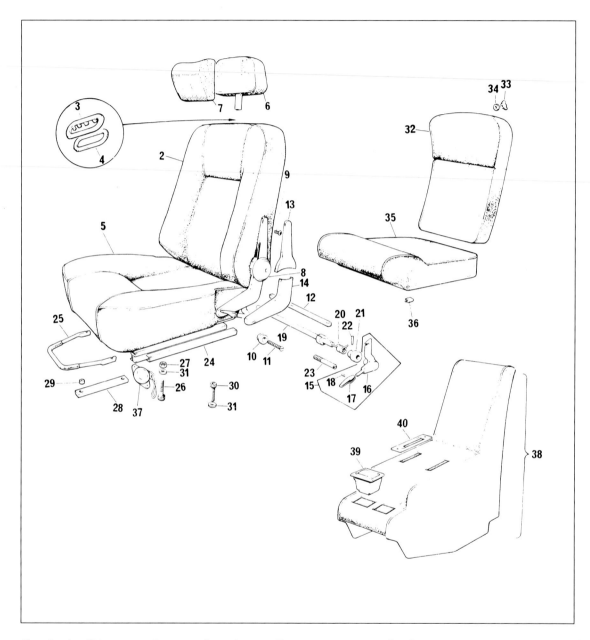

Comfort is all-important in a grand-touring car. Interceptor seats used to be made of Dunlopillo and, apart from the sheepskin inserts of certain US export models, covered in Connolly leather. Although Dunlopillo was extremely comfortable, it was prone to splitting after a long period, and fire regulations outlawed it in favour of dense modern foam cushion. The latest Interceptor seats are designed to a Recaro pattern.

With care and attention, an Interceptor interior can last indefinitely; trim and upholstery restorations can be carried out at the factory.

1	Front seat assy LH – c/w headrest	10	Pivot pin – recliner to cushion	19	Rod assy – seat retainer mech.	30	Screw – socket hd. – seat to chassis
2	Front seat squab assy	11	Screw – recliner to cushion	20	Spring – seat retainer mech.	31	Washer – plain
3	Location plate – headrest	12	Connecting rod – recliner mech.	21	Cover cap – rod	32	Rear seat squab assy RH/LH
4	Reinforcement – location plate	13	Finisher – recliner RH/LH – upper	22	Pin – taper groove – rod	33	Wing nut – squab to body
5	Front seat cushion assy RH/LH	14	Finisher – recliner RH/LH – lower	23	Stop bar – retaining hook handle	34	Washer – plain
6	Headrest assy	15	Retaining hook assy – seat RH/LH	24	Seat slide assy RH/LH	35	Rear seat cushion RH/LH
7	Headrest pillow assy	16	Retaining hook RH/LH	25	Handle – seat slide	36	Clip – cusion covering to frame
8	Seat recliner mech. (Plain/adj.) – RH/LH side – RH/LH seat	17	Handle – retaining hook	26	Screw – socket hd. – slide to seats	37	Switch – safety belt warning
9	Screw – recliner to squab	18	Screw – handle to hook	27	Locknut	38	Console assy – rear seat
				28	Packer – front seat	39	Ash tray – console
				29	Bush – packer	40	Bezel – seat-belt – rear console

bolt it on to a 440 block. This was not possible previously, as the Hemi heads had got different pushrods and valve angles, plus the water passages didn't match up. Now they've arranged the heads so that they basically fit straight on. Hugh Wainwright's car was in a sense the guinea pig, and what a car it proved to be. There was rather more power than the chassis could handle, so a certain amount of attention was required in the suspension and handling department.

John Page was busy getting the cars through the homologation tests, the emission tests, noise tests, and so on. Jensen had to get involved in these areas to some extent back in 1974–75 when cars that were shipped to the US had to be emissions-tested for America, and they had air pumps and catalysts and ran on lead-free fuel. So they learned a little bit then. But things have advanced since, and the European emissions laws were set to become almost as strict as the American ones in 1992. The fuel injection engine then in use already had an air pump and Jensen were trying a catalytic converter on it as well. Without a certificate, these cars couldn't have been sold, so they had to be made to work.

As I wrote this in 1990, there was talk of a new Jensen for 1992, probably with a Chevrolet engine, which Jensen would have bought complete from GM with all their emissions equipment on it. The problem with the then-current engine was that it was the only V8 still made by Chrysler, and it was built in Mexico and used in pick-up trucks. It was scheduled for phasing out in 1991, since Chrysler were switching to V6 and V4 units, so that particular source of engines was about to dry up anyway. Assuming you had to have a big stock V8 power plant, the only American engines big enough to drive this weight of car were Ford or GM. Chevrolet had a suitable 5.7-litre fuel-injected engine, with electronic management system, a six-speed gearbox, and

an alternative four-speed automatic transmission, which Jensen could have used. Hugh Wainwright was already negotiating with Chevrolet, and they seemed keen to get involved. But it turned out that this was all speculative, and the new-design Interceptor never appeared in the metal. Had it done, its construction would have been based on EU stipulations for type approval.

The company did extensive research as regards a new Interceptor. There was no designer within the company, in the sense that Eric Neale was employed in the C-V8 days, and the new car was going to be designed in Chester by a contact of Hugh Wainwright's. Some drawings were prepared, and Jensen staff helped build a prototype, based on the traditional Interceptor back end merged with a new front end, ready to take a Chevrolet engine. The prototype was sent to Chester in the late 1980s, and was never seen again. It differed fundamentally from the Mark IV Interceptor in many ways – the engine bay was quite different from the bulkhead forward to accommodate the Chevrolet engine. The chassis tubes were replaced by a tubular space-frame, which was potentially just as strong. The same front suspension was used, but that's about all; a De Dion set-up was going to be designed for the rear end. The car would have to have been crash-tested, but it should have been satisfactory if it was all triangulated properly and safely.

EUROPEAN REQUIREMENTS

As with the re-manufacture of the Interceptor back in 1982–84, the need for type approval for the construction of a new car was problematic, and when the Mark V Interceptor was mooted, it wasn't known what the EU regulations would be in 1992. At the time, Wainwright was dubious that complete agreement on a single standard

The 1988 Mark IV Coupe, fitted with the front chin spoiler. Purists might also argue that this concession to contemporary aesthetics does very little to enhance or update the appearance of the Interceptor. However, far from being a gimmick, the air dam does actually improve aerodynamics, and the car's frontal aspect has always needed a stronger identity, which the device also provides.

would be reached particularly quickly between member countries. Manufacturers would be divided into three categories: those producing up to fifty vehicles, which is really only the kit-car makers, and where each car has to be inspected individually; those building up to 200 units a year, which Wainwright said would include Jensen, along with Ferrari, Lotus, Morgan and Aston-Martin; and the third category would obviously be for the mass producers.

It would not be necessary to crash-test cars in the middle category but only to hand in their technical specifications. Because most of these cars were using proprietary equipment anyway, Wainwright thought it should be relatively easy to satisfy the requirements. However, if the US specifications were at variance with Europe, it might have been the case that Jensen built a car for the European market rather than making the US its priority. Wainwright believed that in the long term there was a good case for building a Jensen in the USA for the American market, but it was not to be.

A Mark II, a J-Series Mark III Interceptor and a Convertible at Chiswick House.

Curvature of the Convertible and Coupe rear wing makes panel fitting with the boot-lid difficult to get right.

The Interceptor door handles remain the same.

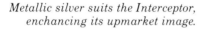

Metallic silver suits the Interceptor, enchancing its upmarket image.

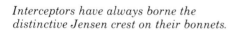

Interceptors have always borne the distinctive Jensen crest on their bonnets.

The smooth, curved and contoured rear-light cluster of the Jensen Interceptor.

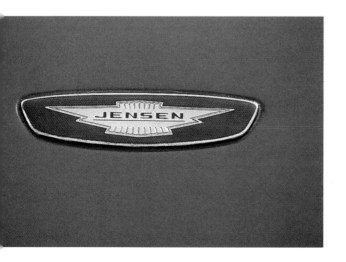

AESTHETICS

It is difficult to decide in aesthetic terms which of the Interceptors is the best-looking design. The archetypal Saloon with its huge glass rear-end works superbly from virtually all angles, and there is a satisfying logic about the way the rear-window glass sweeps down to meet the back panel just above the waist line. The overall impression is one of restrained ostentation, of subdued opulence – an imposing car, it is the product of a high-class Italian styling house, and therefore it could never be described as brash or vulgar; rather, it veers towards the stately and dignified, and its presence demands attention because of its very size.

The grille and nose of the Interceptor up to the Mark IV have always seemed somewhat sparse stylistically; a corporate device like the BMW kidneys or the Alfa Romeo shield would have been welcome, and the Mark IV has the benefit of the air-dam, which, whether or not it confers any practical benefit, lends greater frontal aspect to the car. The stainless-steel sill strip looks out of place today.

The boot and rotund rear-end treatment of both the Coupe and Convertible are well executed, giving these models a totally different character to the grand-touring look of the Saloon. The Coupe's brown-tinted hoop may have gone down well in 1975, but it looks fussy and perhaps even downright gimmicky today. Without that, it would be a more harmonious design than the Saloon, and it is the Convertible, seen with its hood up, which takes the first prize in that respect.

5 The Jensen FF

BACKGROUND TO FOUR-WHEEL DRIVE

The story of the Jensen FF goes back to 1950, when Irish tractor-maker Harry Ferguson formed a research company with racing drivers Freddie Dixon and Tony Rolt. The difference between Ferguson's approach to four-wheel drive and other systems was that previous models were largely agricultural or military-orientated, whereas Harry Ferguson Research was intent on producing a four-wheel-drive passenger car. The principle of four driven wheels is a sound one, since traction is available to such a vehicle in some of the very worst driving conditions – you can go places in a four-wheel drive car in circumstances that make a conventional two-wheel-drive car downright lethal, and the controllability of the four-wheel-drive car verges on the uncanny.

Added to this are considerations of safety at high speed, because the traditional under-steering characteristics of a front-engined four-wheel-drive car are easily controlled by steering input; less effort is involved, and the car's behaviour in fast bends is more predictable as forces brought to bear on the tyres are halved. There is also a gain in weight distribution in a car of this layout, and tyre wear is reduced by being more evenly spread between all four wheels.

Much was expected of the Ferguson P99 four-wheel-drive Grand Prix car but, although Stirling Moss won the Oulton Park Gold Cup event with the car in 1961, it proved heavy and over complex for competition at this level, and progressed not a great deal further. Innes Ireland and Graham Hill tried the car during the Tasman series of 1962–63, but found its handling somewhat outdated. Things progress fast at that level of motor sport. Ferguson lent the P99 to Peter Westbury, reigning hill-climb champion, for the 1964 season, and Westbury took the title again in what was basically the same 1961 car.

Meanwhile, Ferguson continued to develop their own system for four-wheel-drive passenger cars, using their own prototype which looked like a cross between a MkI Jaguar and a Rover 90. They were also trying a flat-four engine, plus a torque converter following the principles of the Italian Count Teramala. Pitted against a variety of cars from Zephyr and Vanguard to VW and Herald, the Ferguson prototype ran rings round all of them in off-road tests and skid-pan conditions.

The Ferguson P99 design reappeared at Indianapolis in 1964, in enlarged form, where it was run with a 500bhp Novi V8 engine by Andy Granatelli and STP, running well in qualifying, but eliminated in a second-lap accident. The next racing team to try four-wheel-drive was BRM, and here the engine was mounted behind the driver, which was by now the accepted layout for a racing car. It was felt at the time that the car was too much of a lash-up, being only ever regarded as a test bed; it features only once, in practice for the 1964 Grand Prix at Brands Hatch.

Hill-climber Peter Westbury built his own Felday-BRM sports racing car, incorporating the Ferguson four-wheel-drive system, and

(Overleaf) The world's first four-wheel-drive production car. FF specification included aircraft-derived Dunlop-Maxaret anti-lock brakes.

enjoyed a degree of success at club level at the end of 1965–66. At the same time, Ferguson were involved with Bruce McLaren in developing a Ferguson-Teramala torque converter, to be used instead of a conventional gearbox, in his McLaren-Oldsmobile Group 7 Can-Am car.

After that it was not until 1969 that Team Lotus contested both Indianapolis 500 with the Lotus 64 and the Lotus 63 in Formula 1. This was at a time when aerofoils were very much in their infancy and had the habit of coming adrift with cataclysmic results, and tyre technology was not particularly advanced; four-wheel drive seemed the best way to go.

The 64 proved fast in qualifying at Indianapolis but Mario Andretti's car crashed due to a broken rear-hub failure, and the three cars were withdrawn. When Jochen Rindt drove the Lotus 63 into second place, again at Oulton Park in the Gold Cup, he pronounced himself dissatisfied with the spread of power from front to rear, whilst Graham Hill had reported poor handling at Zandvoort. Mario Andretti found it just plain slow at Watkins Glen and, although the McLaren and Matra teams built four-wheel-drive F1 cars that season, it was realized that the concept was just too cumbersome in cars where power-to-weight ratio is so crucial. Rallying, of course, was a different matter, for maximum traction is all.

Besides Jensen, other companies to apply the four-wheel-drive logic in those early days of the 1960s were the Ford Motor Company, who supplied some thirty Mark III Zephyr-Zodiacs to the police, going on to produce a four-wheel-drive competition version of the 3-litre Capri. In 1980 came the Audi quattro, which started life as the brainchild of Audi Chief Engineer, Dr Ferdinand Piech. A major shareholder in Porsche, Piech had masterminded their mighty 917 sports-racing car of the late 1960s. In 1977 he was set to turn a humble Audi 80 into the World Rally Championship winner. Using the 80 as a test bed, and drawing on experience from the company's Iltis off-roader, the concept took shape under Chassis Engineer Jorg Bensinger, with ex-Mercedes competitions engineer Hans Nedvidek sorting out the complexities of permanent four-wheel-drive transmission to get everything into a more compact unit suitable for a conventional family car.

Audi had plenty of precedents to go on for the quattro, apart from the Jensen FF: there were World War II jeeps and Land-Rovers, of course, and DKW's 1956 Munga and Audi's 1976 Iltis off-roaders were the parent company's own first steps into four-wheel drive. Going pre-war, Dr Ferdinand Porsche had already designed a four-wheel-drive Beetle, as well as the early post-war mid-engined 4WD Cisitalia Grand Prix car; it was the sporting potential of four-wheel drive which appealed to Piech and Bensinger, not only because they believed superior traction could win races, but in the final analysis, a successful competition programme with four-wheel drive would demonstrate the system's worth and thus sell more cars.

It was not until Audi launched the quattro Turbo that the world at large started to catch on to the advantages of four-wheel drive and, really, another ten years would pass before rallying results made it essential for manufacturers to list a four-wheel-drive model in their catalogue.

JENSEN GOES 4WD

Harry Ferguson died in 1960, but not before the Ferguson system had matured; the breakthrough came when Technical Director Claude Hill produced an effective front-rear torque-split differential. They also created a vehicular application for the Dunlop Maxaret anti-lock braking system, previously developed for retarding the progress of landing and taxiing aircraft. Bearing in mind the team's bias towards motor racing, it is hardly surprising that their efforts were directed that way.

However, a deal was done with the ever-forward-looking Jensen in 1962, where the Ferguson system would be fitted to a C-V8. In order to house the central differential and transfer casing, it was necessary to lengthen the C-V8 FF's chassis and body by 4in (102mm). In fact the C-V8 FF got a chassis all to itself, built in typical boots-and-braces style of two box sections which narrowed inwards towards the front of the car, braced by a rigid floorpan and 5in (127mm) steel outrigger tubes, which together with a pair of 4in tubes extending rearwards, supported the heavy glassfibre body. To cope with the extra loads on the front suspension and drive-train, an additional sub-frame was installed. Whilst the suspension set-up at the rear was unchanged from the regular C-V8, the front coil-spring and wishbone arrangement was altered so that the front drive-shafts were straddled by double coil-springs.

FERGUSON FORMULA

FF stood for Ferguson Formula, the ingredients of the formula being Claude Hill's master differential, which allowed a torque split of 37 per cent front to 67 per cent rear. It worked in conjunction with a pair of one-way clutches, and was driven off the Torqueflite gearbox; the rear prop shaft was operated by the master differential, and the front output shaft worked by a Morse Hy-vo chain system. The function of the one-way clutches was significant. Of the two clutches, that governing the front wheels was geared to run faster than the main shaft, allowing the front wheels to override the back ones by 16.5 per cent. In addition, it controlled front wheel-spin under load and together with the Maxaret system, prevented the rears locking up under braking. Conversely, the slower running clutch permitted the back wheels to

overrun the fronts by 5.5 per cent, and controlled rear traction under load, and the front end under braking.

Coupled to the four-wheel-drive control box and the master differential, the role of the Maxaret unit was to sense the average retardation of all four road wheels. If it detected loss of traction through a wheel starting to lock up, perhaps under heavy braking on a slippery surface, it would alert the brake servo by an electrical signal. A solenoid-controlled valve in the servo would shuttle a vacuum from one side of the diaphragm to the other, giving progressive deceleration and setting up a pulsing through the braking system, which informed the driver via the brake pedal that he was on a slippery surface.

The C-V8 FF was something of a test bed, for these were early days for four-wheel drive, especially taking into account the power to be transmitted to the road. During testing it was found that the sliding splines of the driveshafts were prone to bind under full power, jamming the suspension in the process, so the prototype was fitted with pot-type cv joints instead, which coped with the tendency of the shaft to move within the inner joint. The car was actually not quite finished when it was displayed at the 1965 Motor Show. But it naturally generated enormous interest and publicity for the company.

Other superficial differences between the C-V8 and the FF variant were the air vent in the lower front wing and the FF badge on the rear panel. Commenting on the fruits of the Jensen-Ferguson liaison in *Motor Sport* magazine in 1966, Denis Jenkinson observed, 'Although there are no signs of four-wheel drive being accepted as the conventional, there are definite indications that progress is being made in the battle to break down conservative thought in automobile engineering and, on balance, Ferguson Research would seem to have made more rapid progress than either Dr Rumpler (Daimler Benz) or Dr Porsche.'

Twin air-vents identify the FF; the Interceptor has a single, broader vent.

Seen in profile, the extra length of the FF chassis becomes apparent; the second air-vent on the front wing identifies the FF.

FF badging marks the model out as something special.

Models of the Interceptor are rare. This is Dinky Toys' $\frac{1}{43}$rd scale FF Mark I, made in 1968, and featuring opening doors and bonnet. It is a particularly good copy, especially in profile. The only other die-cast model was by Solido.

THE JENSEN FF

The Interceptor-based FF was launched at the 1966 Earls Court Motor Show to international acclaim. *Car* magazine voted it Car of the Year in 1967. From the windscreen backwards, it was essentially the same car, but forward of the engine, the chassis had been lengthened by an extra 9in (229mm). Visually this was almost undetectable, but the one significant external difference between standard Interceptor and FF was the second air vent in the front wings behind the wheelarch of the FF.

The FF needs the extra 9in (229mm) from the bulkhead forward to make room for the front differential and the front brake shafts. Naturally, there had to be space in front of the engine for the differential to sit. The engine is in the same place as the standard Interceptor's, but it was necessary to obtain some more room to get the drive out to the front wheels. Also, the engine was slanted up and canted over to the left to make room for the prop-shaft to come forwards and drive the differential. The extra 9in (229mm) is in the chassis tubes. It was also necessary to widen the chassis and relocate the rails on the outside of the car because of the positioning of the four-wheel-drive unit.

The FF chassis tubes run down the outside of the car and then turn in at right angles between the wheelarches. Only one Convertible was ever turned into an FF – and this from a second-hand car – and its chassis was found to be a little more flexible at the rear, because of the absence of the central chassis tubes.

It is common practice today for four-wheel-drive manufacturers to cast everything in the sump, and components are all smaller and more refined, but in 1966 it was quite a breakthrough in passenger transport. No FFs have been made since 1972, and it was only the fact that they couldn't be converted to left-hand drive that brought progress to a halt. It is probably true that if they could have been converted successfully and sold in the US, FFs would have outsold the Interceptor in the end.

The FF was costly to produce, and was often seen as a mobile PR exercise; yet there continued to be insufficient appreciation of the potential of four-wheel drive. Despite the Car-of-the-Year accolade, it was only ever going to be built in right-hand-drive form, and nobody in Europe or the US wanted it. If enough money had been thrown at it, anything might have been possible, but at the time, the Jensen coffers weren't exactly overflowing with money. They tried several methods of transferring the steering gear to the left, including a chain-drive system of which Roland Emmett would have been proud, but there was no satisfactory answer.

Nowadays FFs are in great demand. People spend more money having their FFs restored than any other Interceptors, because of their rarity, but they were not necessarily any better built than the Interceptor. One FF has perhaps more of a chequered history than most. In January 1966, the Porsche factory ordered an FF through their UK Concessionaires, AFN Ltd. Clearly there was a waiting list at the time, for Porsche didn't get the car, chassis 119/008, until June the following year. The two-tone grey FF was then used for research work at Porsche's own Weissach testing ground, and after a mere 2,253 miles, (3,625km) they reported the failure of the near-side front hub and drive-shaft, but there was no warranty claim from Porsche, and the car was returned to the UK in 1969, where it was registered and sold on. The car currently belongs to Walter Scott.

It is not altogether clear what Porsche were doing with the FF, although it is quite natural for a high-tech company like Porsche to be interested in what was at the time the only four-wheel-drive road car available outside the Land-Rover and Jeep segment. We have already seen how Ferdinand Piech was heavily involved with Porsche's competition programme at the time, which

A handsome beast by any standards, the Mark II FF combined superb traction and handling with a luxurious interior.

The Mark II FF's fascia included rocker switches instead of the Mark I's toggles; all auxiliary gauges were now in line above the central console.

An FF and assorted Interceptors awaiting maintenance or restoration in the West Bromwich factory car-park.

Mark II FF with bonnet air-intake; the headlights are closer together than the Interceptor's.

From the rear, FF II styling is restrained, yet refined.

An FF newly arrived for maintenance at the factory.

centred on the 917 sports-racing cars and, as Audi's Technical Director, a decade later, he would instigate the development and production of the Audi quattro. However, as a consequence of the Porsche experience, Jensen Motors had to modify a number of FFs with different bearings in the front hubs. Perhaps the closest expression of the FF concept in today's terms is the Porsche Carrera 4, which costs £54,000 at the time of writing.

EVOLUTION OF THE FF

The Mark II FFs received the same trim and upholstery changes as their two-wheel-drive stable-mates. From October 1969, they were now priced at £7,705, and their attributes came in for some close scrutiny now that the competition was hotting up in the shape of the Aston Martin DBS and relatively bargain-basement Jaguar XJ-6. Some people were dubious of the validity of the FF's four-wheel-drive layout, particularly now the Selectarides had been replaced with non-adjustable dampers set at the old units' third click. The cars were said to be less stable, the handling less precise, although their ability in adverse weather conditions was still way ahead of the game; and in performance terms, the FF could still get to 60mph (100kph) in 7.4 seconds and reach 100mph (160kph) in a fraction under 20 seconds, topping out at 140mph (225kph).

With the inception of the Mark III Interceptor and the new top-of-the-range SP model in October 1971, the costly FF's days were numbered, and in fact only seventeen cars bearing the FF Mark III badge left the factory. Total production of FFs reached a mere 320 units, broken down into 196 FF Mark Is, and 107 FF Mark IIs and seventeen Mark III FFs. It was a sad and rather inconsequential end to a highly innovative car, and was, in a sense, the harbinger of the demise of the whole company, looming only five years away.

This flat landscape emphasizes the long, low profile of the 1967 Mark I FF.

Factory picture of the FF II, introduced in October 1969, and capable of 0–60mph (0–100kph) in 8.1 seconds and a top speed of 141mph (226.9kph). Despite this capability, a contemporary road test in Autocar *suggested that the FF's traction was so impressive that the engine ran out of steam on a race circuit.*

Carrying out maintenance work on an FF is quite a different matter from a regular Interceptor. It's heavy work; dismantling a gearbox is described as 'arm-wrenching' by Andrew Edwards at Cropredy Bridge Garage. The advantage of such sturdy engineering is that it just doesn't break. The only components Cropredy have ever replaced in a transfer gearbox have been a drive-chain and an oilseal, which may well be a reflection on the FF transmission's agricultural origins.

The FF was an astonishing car to drive in bad conditions; it was remarkably efficient, and something of an enigma, being a luxury car weighing two tons, with 300bhp 7.2-litre engine and automatic transmission, blithely going about its business in the snow-covered hills; Edwards even towed a Range Rover out of a ditch with an FF under these conditions.

ROADHOLDING

The FF is a heavy car, and it lumbers slightly when cornering on B roads, despite power steering, but once on an open section, off it goes. There are no dramas, just certain solid surge. The power builds up steadily, and you soon run out of opportunities to see what it is really capable of. On the bendy sections, the FF doesn't respond to variations of the throttle to adjust its line through the bends, like a two-wheel-drive car might; you have to use the steering wheel to drive it through, and this could seem uncanny at first. Once you're used to it, it is particularly confidence-boosting.

In this respect, if you follow another car into a bend, you know that all being well, you will be able to power past it as soon as the road ahead is clear for a hundred yards or so. You would have to be trying very hard on the road to make the FF step out of line. In adverse weather conditions, traction is in a different league. Whereas a regular rear-drive car would be all over the place, in an entertaining sort of way, the FF would go, quite nonchalantly, exactly where you wanted it to. There was certainly nothing else on the market to touch it, and over twenty years later, it is still impressive when the going gets tough.

Numbers produced of Jensen series

S-type:	20 approximately	
H-type:	6 approximately	
HC-type:	6 approximately	
PW:	17	
Interceptor 6-cylinder:	57	Saloon
	30	Cabriolet
	1	Sedanca de Ville
	88	
541 Series		
Standard	169	RHD Manual
De Luxe	53	RHD Manual (includes one V8-engined car)
Prototypes	4	RHD Manual (includes two Convertibles)
	226	
541R	150	DS5 engine RHD Manual (includes one with automatic gearbox)
	43	DS7 engine RHD Manual
	193	
541S	104	RHD Manual (includes one fitted later with V8 engine)
	20	RHD Manual
	3	Experimental
	127	
C-V8 Series		
Mk I	67	RHD Auto
	1	Experimental
	68	
Mk II	232	RHD Auto
	7	RHD Manual
	8	LHD Auto
	3	Experimental
	250	
Mk III	176	RHD Auto
	2	RHD Manual
	2	LHD Auto
	1	Experimental
	181	

Interceptor Series
Saloon:

Mk I	924	RHD Auto
	22	RHD Manual
	45	LHD Auto
	1	LHD Manual
	32	LHD Auto motorized chassis supplied to Vignale
	1,024	

Mk II	694	RHD Auto
	432	LHD Auto
	1	Experimental
	1,127	

Mk III	3,500 approximately
Convertible	467 approximately
SP:	467 approximately
Coupe:	54 approximately

Mk IV	13	Convertible
	4	Saloons
	1	Fixed head (Coupe)
	18	

FF:

Mk I	195	RHD Auto

Mk II	109	RHD Auto
	1	Experimental
	110	

Mk III	15	RHD Auto

Jensen Healey Series

Prototypes	9
Mk I	3,349 approximately
Mk II	7,146 approximately

Jensen GT	290	LHD
	217	RHD
	507	

ROAD TEST
Jensen FF (6,276 c.c.)

Reproduced from *Autocar*

MANUFACTURER
Jensen Motors Ltd., West Bromwich, Staffordshire.

PRICES

Basic	£4,707	15s	0d
Purchase Tax	£1,309	15s	10d
Total (in G.B.)	£6,017	10s	10d

EXTRAS (inc. PT)

Cibie quartz-iodine fog lamps (fitted)	£19	14s	8d

PERFORMANCE SUMMARY

Mean maximum speed	130 mph
Standing start ¼-mile	15.9 sec
0-60 mph	8.4 sec
30-70 mph (through gears)	7.7 sec
Typical fuel consumption	14 mpg
Miles per tankful	224

At-a-glance: Unique four-wheel-drive GT. Big, lazy American engine gives sparkling performance. Smooth automatic transmission, slow to change down. Almost unlimited traction and incredible roadholding from Ferguson 4-wd system. Anti-lock braking not yet perfect. Well equipped and comfortable four-seater.

Advertised as 'the world's most advanced car' and with a price tag slightly more than £6,000, the Jensen FF seems formidable at first acquaintance. Its 16ft length and angular Italian styling make it impressive (to say the least) as it sits by the kerb, and the deep throb of its 6.3-litre vee-8 engine suggests there is power to spare. In themselves, these qualities are not so unusual; but under the skin there is something much more, something unique that makes this the safest high performance car available today: four-wheel drive and anti-lock braking.

When we first drove the Oldsmobile Toronado we were apprehensive about how a large American car would behave with front-wheel drive. We were surprised at how much earlier the 500 lb.ft. of torque could be applied in a bend and how controllable, and therefore safe, the Toronado was. Steering the Jensen FF into a corner is uncanny, because the car seems to pull itself round with a combination of all the best front-drive and rear-drive characteristics. It is as much in advance of the Toronado as the Toronado is ahead of the rear-drive Americans.

All this is the natural result of transmitting drive to all the wheels, but if it were as simple as just that there would be far more four-wheel drive cars in production. Ferguson Research have taken many, many years to develop the split-torque system to the present state where it is sufficiently viable for Jensen to put it into production and for a converted Ford Mustang to be under active assessment for police work by the Swedish Government. After almost 3,000 miles of testing in England and on the Continent, we feel the Ferguson Formula four-wheel drive gives the Jensen a tremendous advantage.

To recap on the fundamentals, the FF has a tubular chassis welded to its steel-panelled body, with a live rear axle and double-wishbone front suspension. The engine and automatic gearbox come from Chrysler and the integrated all-disc anti-lock braking system has been developed by Ferguson Research and is made jointly by Dunlop and Girling. At the back of the gearbox is a differential which splits the torque in a ratio of 37:63 per cent between the front and rear wheels. There is a standard Salisbury rear axle and at the front a chassis-mounted differential with double-jointed drive shafts; the front propeller shaft passes along the left-hand side of the engine and gearbox.

Just over a year ago we tested the two-wheel drive Jensen Interceptor, which is exactly the same as the FF except that it has no four-wheel drive and is therefore a little shorter in the wheelbase. This was a truly dynamic car with a top speed of 133mph and a 0 to 100mph

PERFORMANCE

SECONDS

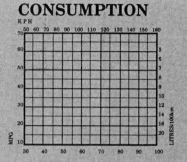

MAXIMUM SPEEDS

Gear	mph	kph	rpm
Top (mean)	130	209	5,080
(best)	130	209	5,080
Intermediate	88	142	5,000
Low	52	84	5,000

Standing ¼-mile 15.9 sec 86 mph
Standing Kilometre 29.3 sec 111 mph

CONSUMPTION

KPH

TIME IN SECONDS	3.1	4.4	6.2	8.4	10.8	13.8	17.5	22.5	28.2	37.2
TRUE SPEED MPH	30	40	50	60	70	80	90	100	110	120	130
INDICATED SPEED	31	42	52	63	73	83	94	104	115	126	136

Mileage recorder 1.7 per cent over-reading.
Test distance 2,922 miles.

SPEED RANGE, GEAR RATIOS AND TIME IN SECONDS

mph	Top (3.07-6.76)	Inter (4.45-9.79)	Low (7.52-16.55)
10-30	–	–	2.2
20-40	–	–	2.6
30-50	4.8	3.8	3.2
40-60	5.6	3.8	–
50-70	6.3	4.6	–
60-80	6.9	5.0	–
70-90	7.3	5.5	–
80-100	8.3	6.5	–
90-110	10.7	–	–
100-120	15.1	–	–

HOW THE CAR COMPARES

Maximum Speed (mean) mph

110	120	130	140	150
Jensen FF				
Aston Martin DB6				
Jaguar E-type 2 2				
Jensen Interceptor				
Porsche 911S				

0-60 (sec)

20	10
Jensen FF	
Aston Martin DB6	
Jaguar E-type 2 2	
Jensen Interceptor	
Porsche 911S	

Standing Start ¼-mile (sec)

30	20
Jensen FF	
Aston Martin DB6	
Jaguar E-type 2 2	
Jensen Interceptor	
Porsche 911S	

FUEL

(At constant speeds–mpg)
30 mph	21.9
40	21.9
50	20.6
60	19.3
70	16.6
80	14.8
90	13.1
100	11.5

Typical mpg	14 (20.2 litres/100km)
Calculated (DIN) mpg	15.1 (18.7 litres/100km)
Overall mpg	13.6 (20.8 litres/100km)

Grade of fuel, Super Premium, 5-star (min 100 RM)

OIL

Miles per pint (SAE 20W/40) . . . 600

TEST CONDITIONS Weather: Cloudy, fine. Wind: 0-5 mph. Temperature: 0 deg. C. (32 deg F). Barometer: 29.3in. Hg. Humidity: 78 per cent. Surfaces: Dry concrete and asphalt.

WEIGHT Kerb weight 35.7cwt (3,981lb-1,806kg) (with oil, water and half-full fuel tank). Distribution, per cent F, 52.5; R, 47.5. Laden as tested: 39.3 cwt (4,403lb-1,998kg).

TURNING CIRCLES
Between kerbs L, 39ft 10 in.; R, 39ft 4.5 in.
Between walls L, 41ft 8.5in.; R, 41ft 1in.
Steering wheel turns, lock to lock 3.6

MPG Overall

10	20
Jensen FF	
Aston Martin DB6	
Jaguar E-type 2 2	
Jensen Interceptor	
Porsche 911S	

BRAKES

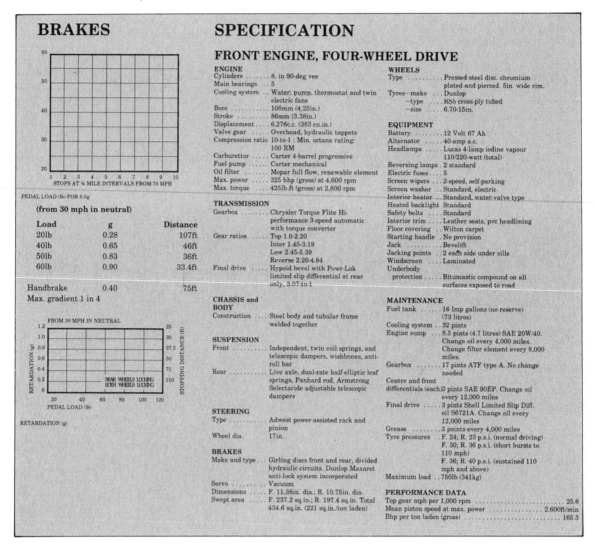

STOPS AT ¼ MILE INTERVALS FROM 70 MPH

PEDAL LOAD (lb) FOR 0.5g

(from 30 mph in neutral)

Load	g	Distance
20lb	0.28	107ft
40lb	0.65	46ft
50lb	0.83	36ft
60lb	0.90	33.4ft

Handbrake	0.40	75ft

Max. gradient 1 in 4

FROM 30 MPH IN NEUTRAL

REAR WHEELS LOCKING
BOTH WHEELS LOCKING

PEDAL LOAD (lb)

RETARDATION (g)

SPECIFICATION

FRONT ENGINE, FOUR-WHEEL DRIVE

ENGINE

Cylinders	8. in 90-deg vee
Main bearings	5
Cooling system	Water; pump, thermostat and twin electric fans
Bore	108mm (4.25in.)
Stroke	86mm (3.38in.)
Displacement	6.276c.c. (383 cu.in.)
Valve gear	Overhead, hydraulic tappets
Compression ratio	10-to-1 : Min. octane rating: 100 RM
Carburettor	Carter 4-barrel progressive
Fuel pump	Carter mechanical
Oil filter	Mopar full flow, renewable element
Max. power	325 bhp (gross) at 4,600 rpm
Max. torque	425lb.ft (gross) at 2,800 rpm

TRANSMISSION

Gearbox	Chrysler Torque Flite Hi-performance 3-speed automatic with torque converter
Gear ratios	Top 1.0-2.20
	Inter 1.45-3.19
	Low 2.45-5.39
	Reverse 2.20-4.84
Final drive	Hypoid bevel with Powr-Lok limited slip differential at rear only, 3.07-to-1

CHASSIS and BODY

Construction	Steel body and tubular frame welded together

SUSPENSION

Front	Independent, twin coil springs, and telescopic dampers, wishbones, anti-roll bar
Rear	Live axle, dual-rate half-elliptic leaf springs, Panhard rod, Armstrong Selectaride adjustable telescopic dampers

STEERING

Type	Adwest power-assisted rack and pinion
Wheel dia.	17in.

BRAKES

Make and type	Girling discs front and rear, divided hydraulic circuits. Dunlop Maxaret anti-lock system incorporated
Servo	Vacuum
Dimensions	F. 11.38in. dia.; R. 10.75in. dia.
Swept area	F. 237.2 sq.in.; R. 197.4 sq.in. Total 434.6 sq.in. (221 sq.in./ton laden)

WHEELS

Type	Pressed steel disc. chromium plated and pierced. 5in. wide rim.
Tyres—make	Dunlop
—type	RS5 cross-ply tubed
—size	6.70-15in.

EQUIPMENT

Battery	12 Volt 67 Ah
Alternator	40-amp a.c.
Headlamps	Lucas 4-lamp iodine vapour 110/220-watt (total)
Reversing lamps	2 standard
Electric fuses	5
Screen wipers	2-speed, self-parking
Screen washer	Standard, electric
Interior heater	Standard, water-valve type
Heated backlight	Standard
Safety belts	Standard
Interior trim	Leather seats, pvc headlining
Floor covering	Wilton carpet
Starting handle	No provision
Jack	Bevelift
Jacking points	2 each side under sills
Windscreen	Laminated
Underbody protection	Bitumastic compound on all surfaces exposed to road

MAINTENANCE

Fuel tank	16 Imp gallons (no reserve) (73 litres)
Cooling system	32 pints
Engine sump	8.5 pints (4.7 litres) SAE 20W/40. Change oil every 4,000 miles. Change filter element every 8,000 miles.
Gearbox	17 pints ATF type A. No change needed
Centre and front differentials (each)	3 pints SAE 90EP. Change oil every 12,000 miles
Final drive	3 pints Shell Limited Slip Diff. oil S6721A. Change oil every 12,000 miles
Grease	3 points every 4,000 miles
Tyre pressures	F. 24; R. 23 p.s.i. (normal driving) F. 30; R. 36 p.s.i. (short bursts to 110 mph) F. 36; R. 40 p.s.i. (sustained 110 mph and above)
Maximum load	750lb (341kg)

PERFORMANCE DATA

Top gear mph per 1,000 rpm	25.6
Mean piston speed at max. power	2.600ft/min
Bhp per ton laden (gross)	165.3

acceleration time of only 19 sec. With extra gears to churn, the FF loses a little of this performance, but not much. Maximum speed was again identical in both directions, at exactly 130mph, and 0 to 100mph took 22.5 sec.

While the FF may lose a bit in a straight line on a dry road, it more than makes up for this on twists and turns of if there is any rain about. After a dry day in the Midlands we drove back to London where there had just been a heavy shower and the streets were in that ulta-greasy state which causes unexpected skids and a lot of crumpled wings.

As one set of traffic lights turned green, we gingerly opened the first pair of carburettor butterflies, expecting wheelspin and possibly some snaking, but the FF simply surged forward as if the road were dry. At the next lights we gave it full throttle and the same thing happened; it was impossible to spin the wheels.

A few days later, we were trying the car on fresh snow in Switzerland, still equipped with ordinary cross-ply Dunlop RS5 high-speed tyres at normal pressures. During a standing start with full power, the rear wheels and the right front one would just spin

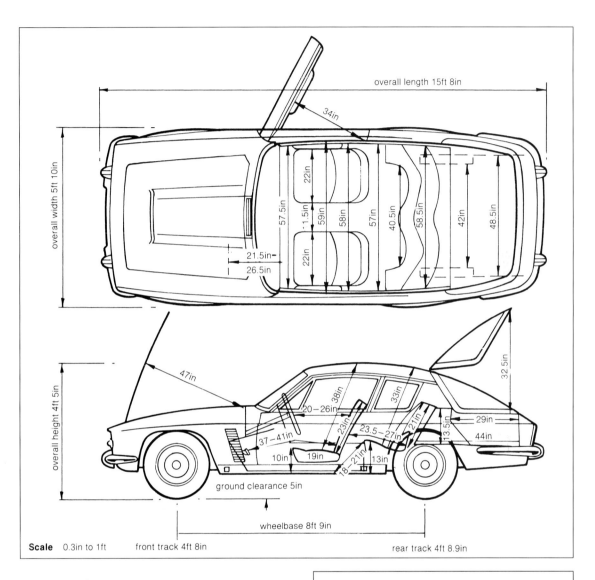

Interceptor dimensions.

Jensen FF Mk II

Leading Dimensions

Overall length	15ft 11in (4,851mm)
Overall width	5ft 9in (1,753mm)
Overall height	4ft 5in (1,346mm)
Wheelbase	9ft 1in (2,769mm)
Track, front	4ft 8⅞in (1,445mm)
Track, rear	4ft 8⅞in (1,445mm)
Ground clearance	5¾in (146mm)
Turning circle	39ft 0in (11,887mm)
Weight	34cwt (1,727kg)

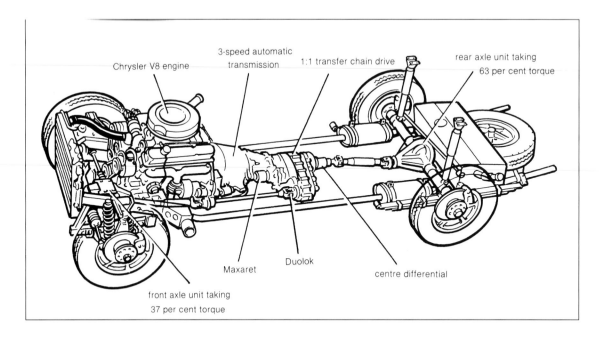

Chrysler V8 engine

3-speed automatic transmission

1:1 transfer chain drive

rear axle unit taking 63 per cent torque

Maxaret

Duolok

centre differential

front axle unit taking 37 per cent torque

Basic layout of the Jensen FF Mark II.

for a moment, but there was enough traction to climb a 1-in-4 nursery ski slope to the total amazement of the piste patrol. Only the rear differential has a Powr-Lok mechanism and there is enough lateral torque reaction at the front when accelerating hard to give the left wheel grip.

All Wheel Control

Cornering the Jensen fast is terribly easy because it seems to steer itself round every turn, exactly on line. Initially the front tyres scrub a bit, particularly on a light throttle, but often this is because the driver has put the lock on too suddenly thinking there would be some understeer. The power-assisted steering takes a little getting used to; it is light and very sensitive with just the right degree of feed-back from the road surface.

Driving to one's accustomed standards, there is always a tremendous margin of spare cornering power in hand. As the dramatic picture we published three weeks ago showed

so well, it looks as if the tyres would pull off the rims of the wheels before the car lost its grip on a dry road. In the wet there may be slightly greater slip angles front and rear, but the balance remains the same and still the FF just goes round each corner on line.

Harking back to the test of the Interceptor, we commented on how well the driver could sense when it would be safe to apply full power without generating a tail slide. With the FF he can floor the accelerator as he enters a blind curve and know the front will always pull in as tightly as required and the back will simply follow round without hanging out. When one becomes used to these character-istics, it is possible to storm along twisty roads at seemingly impossible speeds, barely lifting for the kinks and bends. Passengers though, need breaking in gently to the new phenomenon, or they are liable to become alarmed.

Eventually, and only on snow, we reached the limits of adhesion for the FF. With more torque to transmit, and without enough grip to give full weight transference rearwards, it is the tail of the car which slides first. Smoothly and progressively the rear end swings out, in just the same way as a conventional rear-wheel-drive car would at a much slower speed. The difference, and it is a big one, comes in the correction: because the front wheels are pulling as well as steering, opposite lock is much more effective and the FF straightens up with a quicker response than we have ever experienced.

While we are fully converted to the advantages of four-wheel drive, we must retain our reservations about the Maxaret anti-lock braking system. The way this works is to sense as soon as the wheels are about to lock (and with four-wheel drive they can lock only together) and reverse the action of the vacuum servo to reduce the pressure in the hydraulic lines. Because the servo works directly as assistance to the pedal, the driver feels this action as a firm kicking-back under his foot. Our presso-meter leapt from 60 to 180lb during this cycling.

With the non-Maxaret Interceptor we obtained a maximum retardation on a dry road of 0.9g and we were able to repeat this figure on the FF merely by standing on the pedal and letting the mechanism do its work. With practice on the Interceptor, a skilled driver could hold this g figure for the whole of his stop, whereas on the FF there is nothing he can do but leave himself in the hands of the unit, which pulsates down from this peak and back again. The cycling rate is quite slow, about two or three times a second, which has the advantage of giving better steering control − while the wheels are unlocked − during emergency braking.

On wet roads the pedal kicks back at much lower pressures, because the wheels try to lock earlier. We never achieved the claimed cycling rate of five or six per second though, and we felt the system responses were too slow.

Two or three times the brake pedal kicked back at us without apparent reason when we were braking only gently from high speed. Psychologically it is disturbing to have automatic control take over in a panic situation such as a crash stop, even though the system may be bringing the car to rest in a shorter distance. On this last point we are not yet convinced, and we look forward to carrying out some further more elaborate braking tests at an early opportunity.

Luxury Interior

The rest of the FF is well up to what one has a right to expect for the price. Inside there is sweet smelling Connolly hide; a twin-speaker radio with electric aerial is standard. Windows drop and lift by electric motors and there is an impressive, but not very tidy, array of instruments and switches. On the back window is a new type of heating element which is applied to the inner surface and effectively prevents misting up. It cannot cope with frost or snow on the outside though, since toughened glass is too good a thermal insulator.

Although the heating and ventilating system is comprehensive, with separate hot and cold air ducting, it lacks temperature sensitivity and the short levers poking through the central console panel are stiff to adjust. There is a two-speed booster fan for the hot-air system and a separate single-speed fan for the cold-air inlets, which take the form of adjustable nozzles in the centre and at each end of the facia.

Surprisingly, there is no ignition warning lamp and the indicator tell-tales are too dim and almost hidden under the edge of the padding between the speedometer and rev counter. The horns are far too polite and melodious for a high performance GT, and they do not carry at speed.

Seating is very comfortable, although it is a bit of a struggle to climb in behind the wheel, especially when another car or a wall prevents the wide door from opening fully. Backrest angle can be adjusted and the steering column telescopes to suit different arm *lengths and different driving attitudes. Back seats are well shaped, but the limited dimensions here prevent one getting really comfortable.*

All too often high speed cars are reduced to a crawl at night because of poor lighting equipment. In our Interceptor test we criticized the four headlamp system .and suggested iodine vapour units. These are now standard on both Jensen models, and Lucas are to be congratulated on supplying by far the best set of lamps we have driven behind. Even on dipped beams it is possible to sustain very high speeds in the dark with confidence, and on main beams it is just as though the road ahead is flood-lit.

We have concentrated in this test on the peculiar aspects of the four-wheel drive. The engine and transmission performed faultlessly, although we would have liked less delay in the manual over-ride mechanism. Noise levels were very low, and the FF makes no more fuss at 120mph than it does around town. On the Continent it is truly a grand touring car with a huge appetite for gobbling up the miles, hundreds at a time. In England it is a relaxing car, which gets you there much earlier than you expect. Somehow the big, lazy engine and supreme cornering security with automatic gears and power steering take all the work out of driving and bring back much of the pleasure, despite restrictions and congestion.

6 The Driving Experience

To begin with, the Interceptor is a grand-touring car of the old school; it was a big car in the 1960s and, although it doesn't have the air-dams, skirts and assorted aerodynamic paraphernalia of modern machines, it still looks big today. It cossets just like a grand tourer should. You sink into the generous front seat, and have the sensation of a comprehensive array of instruments and controls around you. Ahead of the steeply-raked windscreen, but not immediately visible because of the low seating position, is the long, long bonnet. Its squareness helps judge its farthest extent when aiming for the apex of a bend, or in a tight parking situation.

The seats are well-shaped but without really giving enough lateral support; this is no doubt improved in the Mark IV cars. The pedals are widely spaced and straight ahead but with no left footrest. Cocooned inside, the passenger is always conscious of travelling in a solidly built vehicle, and there are sufficient permutations to the front seat adjustments to enable the driver to find the optimum driving position. Like most Coupes, there is barely enough space for two adults in the back, unless those in front crouch up against the steering wheel or glove box but, certainly in the front, there is headroom for even a six-footer to sit upright. Apart from some of the very first Vignale-built cars which had vinyl covering their door trims and central consoles, the original cars were fully decked out in leather. Certain US-spec cars had sheepskin panels inset. The front seats recline, and the rear ones are sculpted for individual posteriors — but perhaps all two-plus-two designs should really be considered only as appropriate for two adults

No frills, just clean lines. The rear of the Mark IV Coupe, now with proper saloon roof, is as neat and interesting a piece of car design as you'll find anywhere.

and two children. For some reason, touring cars have never been built with the notion in mind of four adults going very far together.

That's one of the reasons they wanted to try the De Dion rear-end, which would enable the rear bulkhead to be shifted back a few inches to get more rear leg-room. As it is, a live axle bouncing up and down has got to have room. The internal feeling of space is impressive, although perhaps the car's exterior dimensions suggest an even larger interior; none the less, the tall person

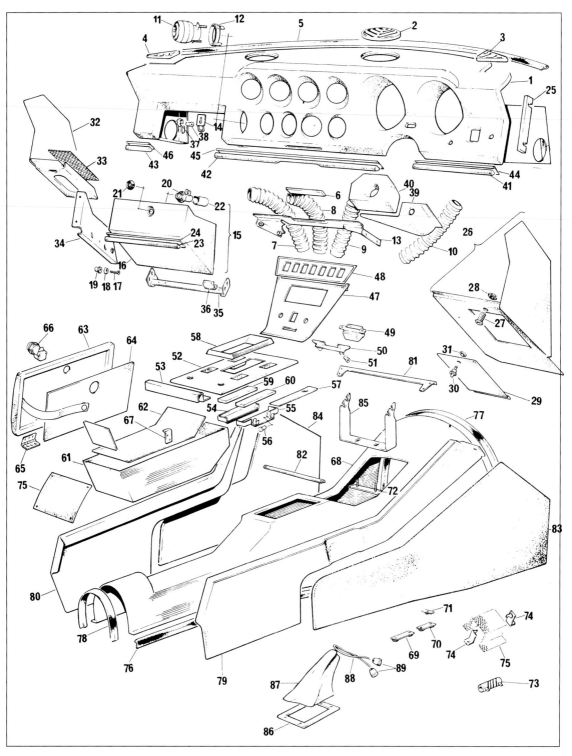

The parts which form the fascia, dashboard, centre console and transmission cover, together with heater pipes; the final effect is somewhat different when all the dials are installed and the interior trimmed with leather, walnut, and Wilton pile.

1 Fascia panel assy	28 Camlock nut	Lear Jet/Voxon/ Cassette Player	gearbox – trimmed
2 Vent – demister – centre	29 Lid assy – fascia closing panel	48 Bezel – switch panel	69 Plate – retaining – long
3 Vent – demister – side RH	30 Camlock stud	49 Relay – fuel filler lid and air-conditioning	70 Plate – retaining – short
4 Vent – demister – side LH	31 Camlock retainer		71 Plate – fixing
5 Seal – fascia	32 Closing panel LH – fascia – RHD	50 Bracket – diverter illumination	72 Mounting plate – Lear Jet
6 Cover – panel light	32 Closing panel RH – fascia – LHD	51 Bulb	73 Resistor – panel light
7 Hose – face level vent – long	33 Mesh – closing panel	52 Gear selector panel (trimmed/ veneered)	74 Bracket – mounting – resistor
8 Hose – face level vent – short	34 Bracket – glove box	53 Bracket assy – selector panel support	75 Cover panel – resistor
9 Hose – demister – centre	35 Strip – hinge – glove box	54 Retainer – gear indicator (positional)	76 Seal – gearbox cover – side
10 Hose – demister – side	36 Hinge – glove box	55 Retainer – gear indicator (numerical)	77 Seal – gearbox cover – front
11 Vent – face level – front	37 Clip – glove-box light	56 Bulb – gear indicator	78 Seal – gearbox cover – rear
12 Bezel – face level vent	38 Bulb	57 Slide – gear selector	79 Console side panel RH
13 Plate – console mounting	39 Cowl – steering column lock	58 Surround – gear lever	80 Console side panel LH
14 Plate – striker – glove-box lock	40 Cowl – steering column	59 Gear selector panel (numerical)	81 Retainer – console – front
15 Glove-box assy	41 Moulding – fascia – driver's side	60 Gear selector panel (positional)	82 Retainer – console – centre
16 Glove box – trimmed	42 Moulding – fascia – centre	61 Companion box assy – less lid	83 Console front panel RH – toe-box inner
17 Stop screw – glove box	43 Moulding – fascia – passenger's side	62 Liner – companion box	84 Console front panel LH – toe-box inner
18 Washer – cup – stop screw	44 Finisher – fascia moulding – driver's side	63 Lid – companion box – less liner	85 Mounting bracket – Lear Jet
19 Rawlnut – stop screw	45 Finisher – fascia moulding – centre	64 Liner – companion box lid	86 Plate – handbrake gaiter
20 Lock – glove box	46 Finisher – fascia moulding – passenger's side	65 Hinge – companion box	87 Gaiter assy – handbrake
21 Escutcheon – lock	47 Switch panel (trimmed-veneered) – for non air-conditioned/air-conditioned cars with Radio-mobile/	66 Lock – companion box	88 Cord – gaiter
22 Cover – lock		67 Plate – striker – lock	89 Acorn – cord
23 Moulding – glove box		68 Cover assy –	
24 Finisher – moulding			
25 Packer – fascia end			
26 Closing panel assy RH – fascia – RHD/LHD			
27 Camlock receptacle			

gratefully acknowledges the generous amount of headroom, and you can sit with your legs almost straight as a front-seat passenger. There is a nice dash layout in the test car, the walnut version from 1974. There are two interior lights and a town or country horn setting.

By today's standards, the Interceptor's suspension is plain old-fashioned, agricultural even, and the cart-sprung rear end shows up its deficiencies on country lanes. Aside from the FF, it doesn't ride or handle as well as a modern Jaguar, but on a fast,

smooth black-top A road, it will be in its element.

The ride is good, solid and firm, on the sporting side of luxury. Koni dampers are fitted nowadays and they help a lot. They gave up using the Selectarides back in the Mark I days, when Armstrong stopped making them. They were quite effective, and it was possible to detect the difference between settings 1 and 4. The test car, an S4, is on 60-series tyres. They are normally on 70-series, and it makes the ride a little bit harsher. Interceptors suffer a little from

Traditional hallmarks of the luxury car: leather upholstery and walnut trim which feature largely in the present-generation Interceptors.

A Mark I Interceptor being put through its paces on an impromptu countryside hill-climb. Generally, the Interceptor was not the sort of car with which you went in for competitions.

Driver's eye view of the Convertible's instrumentation, which was straight from the Mark III; relatively uncluttered, easily readable, and everything within reach.

bump-steer; undulations can tend to throw it off-line a bit, which also has an effect on the live rear axle. Once you upset that heavy rear-end, it takes a few revs for the imbalance to die away.

Like the vast majority of Interceptors, the test car is an automatic; in the normal course of things, you can select D and just drive it, but if the situation demands it, you can hold second for maximum acceleration, and it will go into top on its own; you also get engine braking in second. It feels just like what it is under acceleration: a 140mph (225kph) car. The weight distribution is about 50:50 so the car handles quite well. It will corner pretty flat under power, and there's not much body roll; it reminded me a bit of a Corvette Stingray I was let loose in once at Brands Hatch.

The Interceptor will succumb to roll-oversteer eventually, and in the wet it will understeer, but really, it isn't the sort of machine which you exercise to its ultimate. The Interceptor's appearances on the race track have been conspicuous by their absence. However, it is just as well to be aware of the enormous reserves of power at your disposal when driving one, and if you are trying hard, even if the surface is dry, it is the back end that will go first.

The Interceptor is a heavy car, something belied by the excellent power steering, but the all-round disc brakes are quite up to the job of hauling it down from a high-speed run. There are ventilated discs on the Mark III and solid discs on the Mark II. The trouble with the ventilated discs is that they tend to run too cold, and they require to be caned a bit to get the temperature up.

The test car has an old Radiomobile eight-track stereo system, which was the original fitting. The Lear Jet eight-track was an American version. It was good hi-fi for its time but if anything died a death, it was the eight-track, and a lot of people must have been stuck with a load of tapes. With the current accent on the classic cult and memorabilia, it's swinging back the other way, and people want to keep their car original. But they can't find any tapes to play because most people junked them.

As a motorway cruiser, Interceptors are great. You sit at 70mph (110kph) on a little bit of throttle and you've only got to squeeze it a tad and you can thunder past most people. There's a Green argument for them too, because since 1972 they've been capable of running on lead-free petrol. Being an American engine, when lead-free petrol came in, they all had the appropriate valve-seats installed. Jensen are trying an over-drive unit on it, which, according to John Page, seems to work pretty well. It operates on all three gears, and you can switch it in and out as you please. It's a Laycock unit which a company in the US buys, of which the casing is then adapted to fit into various American gearboxes. It drops the revs by about 800rpm, making for very restful cruising and better fuel economy.

Air-conditioning is particularly useful on cars which have a large glass area, for instance on a misty morning when there's condensation everywhere. You turn the air-conditioning on and it sucks it out; it literally dries the air, and it is important to get the unit checked once every two years or so in case of leaks. The factory never fitted sun-roofs, and never recommended them either, believing that the integrity of the roof structure might be compromised. None the less, a lot of people have had them fitted since, and nobody has had a car collapse yet. Perhaps it was to avoid damaging the splendid pleated leather headlining, which Interceptors always had. Interceptors have been called the 'gentleman's express', which just about sums it up. You can drive it like a sports car, or you can sit back and let it cruise along on its own.

7 End of the Line

From the mid-1980s to the final closure in 1992, the factory was producing one Mark IV Interceptor roughly every ten weeks. The throughput of restorations was greater, and there were at the very least a dozen cars in the various throes of re-fettling at any one time, plus the same again being serviced or having mechanical work done. In addition, the parts service represented probably 40 per cent of Jensen's business, which was a measure of how far the company had come since 1976, when Jensen Parts and Service was all that was left of the firm. A lot of parts were sold to California and New York, as there were plenty of Jensens in the USA. The cars that were in the workshop for service and restoration inevitably had some call on the spares department. Very often, customers left their cars at the factory for three or four months, which allowed sufficient time for them to be taken apart and for whatever work was necessary to be carried out.

Although by 1990 the business had shrunk to a shadow of what it was in its heyday, the feeling of the workforce was still

An Interceptor body in primer. Old-style wheels are used just to manoeuvre the vehicle around the factory; it doesn't matter if they get paint overspray on them.

Mark II headlamp surrounds were in black instead of body colour; overriders were now squared-off instead of pointed.

very positive and the attitude optimistic. From the creation of a chassis to going into paint, it took some 600 to 700 hours. The basis of the chassis was made in the yard outside, the main ladder-frame girders simply mounted on oil drums and welded together. Sophisticated it was not. The chassis was then brought into the factory and placed on a jig, where at least 800 pieces of metal were welded onto it. Constructing the chassis only took a day or so. The panels were shaped on the old presses, some of which were still at Jensen, and some were with outside contractors. Small sections of bodywork were cut by hand, shaped between rollers in what looked like mangles, and welded in place. At that time it took about four weeks to build a complete body. The panels were all welded together in sub-assemblies and then welded on to the chassis. Then the 'door hangers' hung the doors and checked everything over. Next, the sheet-metal workers did all the lead-loading and filing-off. When the Interceptor was in 'volume' production, five people were employed doing the lead-loading and cleaning-off on one car, two people did the quarter panels, and then there were men on the end of the line who rectified any other problems. By 1990, just a handful of specialists built the whole car. Eventually,

the Interceptor went from the assembly line straight to the acid wash to be dipped. This was to remove impurities and provide a good key for the paint.

PAINT JOB

The car spent as much as a week in the paint shop, being given at least six undercoats and as many top coats. Flatting down and polishing removed any runs and orange-peel effect, which could take a long time. In 1990, Jensen introduced a new two-pack paint process to replace the old cellulose finish. This involved removing all the old booths and installing a proper spray room and oven. Most convertibles were finished in red, blue and magnolia; the plain colours tending to show off the lines to better effect.

PRESSED FOR TIME

'It really is a time-consuming job' said Scots sheet-metalworker John Taylor, interviewed in 1990. 'If we had the right tools we could do one panel in five minutes. There are some presses round the back, but most of the tools have either been stolen or were

Rear three-quarter view of the Mark I Interceptor shows it in its more flattering light.

lost to the receiver in 1978, and these are the only large tools we do have.'

So whenever they needed a large panel, they had to send away to somewhere where there was a big enough press. What they made in-house had to be trimmed to shape and then have any necessary holes cut in it. Take a quarter panel, for instance. John Taylor had to cut round it, and cut the wheelarch out. Then he had to make it fit. In an ordinary car factory it would be done on a press, which would stamp it out, and then cut and trim it; everything would be done for him. When it came off the press the panel was ready to put on the car. However, with the hand-to-mouth methodology of the diminished company, the workers had to make everything fit themselves.

Interceptors were expensive because they took a lot of man-hours to produce and that was because there was no money available for tools. 'It would cost a fortune to get the tools you need just to do a little job like I am doing, and you don't need many panels done when you are not on a production line' said Taylor. There were many drawbacks to not having the correct presses as, for example, earlier pressings had to be adapted for later models. Indeed, the Mark III Interceptor rear-light apertures had three holes of differing shapes. Since there were no

presses for Mark I Interceptor rear panels, the Mark III versions had to be adapted by welding in a section of metal, which all had to be finished off properly. With the right press, one would take five minutes.

Taylor described the process: 'To cut out a piece like a quarter panel, we have small machines round the back. We get the patterns down, mark them out on the panel, and then cut them on these machines. With a rotary cutter, it's just a matter of following the line you've marked out. You can bend the panel to get the basic shape, and then you have to manipulate it with hammers, or the tools on the jigs to get it into shape for the stores or fitting on a car.' Hood mechanisms for the Convertible were particularly intricate, as the fifty different parts that made up the linkages all had to be riveted together, with nylon washers at each joint. It was a complex operation, and the entire production run in the company's last days consisted of Convertibles. Up to a point, an Interceptor Coupé would be constructed in the same way, but since there were no roofs, they would have had to be made specially, probably by an outside contractor. Other problematic jobs included fitting screens and, on the Convertible, the drop-light rear three-quarter windows were difficult to install.

8 Restoration

Until the demise of the company in 1992, the Interceptor was kept alive by the reduced workforce, whose principal activity was restoration, the new cars being finished at a rate of one every ten weeks or so.

Although a number of small firms can be found advertising in the *Jensen Owners' Club Magazine*, the garage with the most time-served status and serious commitment to Jensen restoration and maintenance is Cropredy Bridge Garage. The honey-coloured Cotswold stone buildings of this small north Oxfordshire village straddle the Cherwell and its adjacent canal, and a fifty-yard walk from the canal bridge places you amongst a dozen or so highly desirable Jensens. This is the sales forecourt of Cropredy Bridge Garage. Set up and run by Andrew Edwards, the Jensens started to appear there in 1971.

They got started in quite a casual sort of way. One of their regular customers bought an Interceptor, and since there was no one in the area who cared to service anything remotely exotic, he asked them to take care of it. Before then, Cropredy Bridge Garage would look after anything and, for the most part, it was high-performance vehicles. But, having become involved with this one Interceptor, it became apparent to Andrew Edwards that there were relatively few dealers around, and the ones that did exist seemed to be unable or unwilling to get seriously involved with the cars. Consequently, owners were not very keen on going to them. The reason for the dealers' diffidence was in many cases because Jensen was such a small franchise for main-road style garages, and it simply represented a prestigious second fiddle. For Cropredy, this was a bonus, for the customers just poured in from there. Their rates were cheaper too, which has always been a carrot to those who run semi-exotics.

EXPANSION

The original premises expanded to a much larger workshop set back a bit more from the road in 1980, where all the recognized equipment of a vehicle restoration and maintenance operation is much in evidence: two ramps occupied by an Interceptor SP and a Convertible, the former with its sill and side cut away in the throes of major surgery, the latter merely in for a service. A C-V8 restoration nearly finished, the car awaits its bonnet, whilst another C-V8, actually belonging to Andrew Edwards, needs its front end fixing after an accident (which didn't happen while Andrew was driving, he assures us). The most comprehensive restoration in progress when this chapter was written involved a Convertible, which had effectively been completely repanelled. Carrying out the work was Keith Anderson, author and editor of the *Jensen Owners' Club Magazine*. A curious place to find a writer and journalist, you might think, but Keith has always been a Jensen enthusiast, and trained as a car painter.

Keith talked through the build process of the car, and described in his soft Scottish brogue what is involved in the restoration of an Interceptor. The removal of a Coupe's rear screen involves undoing a number of screws and a pair of bolts; the brown glass hoop over the top is gently prised from its bonding with rear and top sections. The back section when

removed reveals the wooden hoop surround-
ing the interior of the rear-scuttle panel,
identifying the car as having started life as a
Convertible; even the mounting points for
the hood can be seen, so clearly the Coupe
was pulled off the Convertible line and then
modified accordingly.

The first places to check for corrosion on
the Interceptor are the stainless-steel covers
over the jacking points. If there is rust there,
it can be calculated to have worked its way
into the entire side member, and a major job
is on the way. As the years go by, of course,
there are more and more areas which need
looking at. The front wheelarches can collect
mud which harbours corrosion-inducing
damp, and both front and rear aprons rot out.
Door bottoms go if the drain channels have
become blocked, as will the bonnet if it's
louvred, for water will seep in and soak the
sound-proofing material. The Interceptor is
such a strong vehicle that there is no danger
of the car banana-ing in the way that a
rusted monocoque convertible might. That
said, the first problem with Interceptor
restoration is rust, although it seems that
glorious chassis has never yet rusted
through, thanks to those great chassis tubes
– at least Cropredy have never had to
replace one yet. They have patched a couple
of back-ends which must have been a bit
weak, but essentially they are the most
reliable bit of metal in the car. The FF is
different, however, and they have replaced a
lot of FF chassis tubes. These do rust badly
because they are in a different position. On
the Interceptor, they are set well into the car,
a foot in from each side. But on the FF they
are right on the edge, and for cosmetic
purposes Jensen put a little oversill on them,
a bit of metal on which to hang that stainless-
steel sill-cover – and if you put two bits of
metal very close together with no protection,
they will sweat, and pick up all the mud and
debris off the road, and corrosion is not far
behind. The chassis tube forms a vacuum and
reservoir for the braking system.

VACUUM RESERVOIR

There is a pipe leading from the servo down
to the offside chassis tube, which is actually
tapped and built into the chassis in a sealed
section of the tube. This acts as a back-up
vacuum reservoir, since Interceptors gobble
up a lot of air under braking, and the servo
just hasn't got enough capacity, hence the
need for a reservoir. But when the chassis
tube rots through in the FF, you lose your
brakes as well, because your servo assistance
is compromised. Cropredy's solution is to
replace the chassis tube, which not
surprisingly is a mammoth task. They have
to be fabricated on the floor from chassis tube
made up by Cropredy Garage themselves.
They buy a tube and then cut it to length,
shape it and then cut it in sections. Although
it is undoubtedly a major job, the artistic
aspect thereof makes it rewarding to do.
Jensen themselves tend to sleeve the chassis
tube; they will put a smaller tube inside the
damaged one, forget about the reservoir
aspect and put a separate vacuum reservoir
in front of the engine.

After tackling any rot in the chassis, it is a
matter of sorting out which panels need
replacing. If a car is particularly bad, then
every one will be changed as a matter of
course. This is where the time and money
aspect rears its ugly head in a big way, for
Keith had been working on the Coupe for
some four months, and the car was still not
yet in primer. When cars are painted at
Cropredy, they certainly look good; there's
not a trace of 'orange peel' to be seen. But
finishing of the bodywork need not be the end
of it, for there is a strong temptation that if
you have to have your engine out for internal
body repairs, you might as well have that
overhauled as well.

Where does it stop? How big is your bank
balance? When the price of a new Interceptor
is the best part of £100,000, does spending
less than half that on a concours restoration
seem out of the way? If you bought your

Mr Shaw, a collector of Aston Martins, was told of a mysterious 'Aston' in a Bournemouth garage. On investigation he discovered it was none other than the Interceptor prototype, and after a year's persuasion, he was able to buy the car from its owner, a garage proprietor who had kept it in storage for some years.

The condition of the prototype Interceptor borders on concours: the interior is original and unmarked.

Since Bryn Shaw acquired the Interceptor prototype in 1987, it has been overhauled mechanically and given a fresh coat of paint. The car is garaged during the winter, but used as everyday transport during the summer months.

The Interceptor prototype has only done 60,000 miles (96,556km) from new.

Interceptor for perhaps £10,000 or £15,000, then maybe it doesn't. Because of what is known now about the whys and wherefores of deterioration in motor cars, and techniques of restoration are now more highly developed, the chances are that a properly restored car will be better than when it was first made. This is not to denigrate the working practices of the factory when the Interceptors were in series production, it's just that the long-term effects of corrosion are better understood today, and are combated accordingly.

For instance, a handful of improvements can be made to the Interceptor during the restoration process. The jacking point covers are made of stainless steel with a mild steel backing plate. The interaction between the two metals promotes corrosion, so the whole item is now made of stainless steel. Some of the electrics are upgraded, because some circuitry was weak, particularly that operating the cooling fan. The wheel studs are replaced because they will have been weakened through use of air-wrenches to tighten the wheel nuts. However, there are several desirable new machines available in the market place for even Jensen restoration money, from Porsche to Jaguar to Mercedes; and build quality is not a problem with cars like these. So, clearly you have to be a keen Jensen *aficionado* and committed to your car to go for a comprehensive rebuild.

Meanwhile, apart from the six or seven Interceptors and 541s for sale on the Cropredy Bridge forecourt, there are equally as many less pristine-looking cars awaiting refurbishment in the yard behind the workshop. For some reason, most of the Interceptors seemed to have been black, although there were other shades, and there is also a handsome 541 which belonged for most of its life to a lady alas barred from driving the car due to old age. Andrew Edwards described it as something of a highlight when she brought the 541 along for service, usually prior to taking off with some of her rowdy friends on the canal in a narrow boat.

OFFICIAL FRANCHISE

Cropredy Bridge Garage became an official Jensen franchise in 1974, and they were doing very well, selling cars and parts, as well as acting as brokers, selling cars on behalf of their owners, despite the fact that it didn't seem to make any sense for a small operation like theirs, tucked away in a Cotswold village, to be dealing in brand-new Jensens. They realized after the collapse that the factory was simply desperate to sell cars from any outlet they could. Cropredy were even buying cars from the receivership and selling them 'like hot cakes' long after Jensen ceased trading. Whereas the main High Street Jensen dealerships had to pack up or revert to another franchise, Cropredy Bridge was small enough and sufficiently flexible to keep going.

They have about 200 customers, with cars built as long ago as 1937. The rest are mostly Interceptors, with a very high proportion of Convertibles against the number made, and a high proportion of FFs against the number made. For some reason they always have five Convertibles going through the works simultaneously; there appears to be no particular reason why there is a succession of soft tops needing restoration. The obvious excuse that careless owners have left the top down in the rain seems unlikely. With the fad for importing allegedly rust-free cars from California, there is a constant trickle of left-hand-drive cars for them to sort out, mostly from dealers. Sometimes owners take fright when given the list of what needs doing to their cars. Edwards produces what amounts to a shopping list of parts and work needed, and the customer can take all of it or just part of it. In the case of an MOT however, there are few compromises if you want the pass certificate.

When I was visiting Cropredy Garage once, I noticed a father and son who were looking pretty despondent. I asked Edwards what the problem was, and it turned out he'd had to quote them £9,000 to get their car through its MOT. They'd bought the Interceptor recently for £11,000, and presented it for its test, the price of which is £14.62p, not anticipating any great problems, apart from perhaps the air-conditioning. Close examination revealed that virtually the entire fabric of the car was rotten, from chassis upwards; the front brake calipers were seized, the handbrake inoperative, and there were other defects with the steering and suspension. They didn't even bother with a compression test. The vehicle was strictly illegal when it was driven away, its owners bent on doing the work themselves, and the episode stands as a salutary lesson in how not to go about buying a second-hand Jensen.

Cropredy Bridge Garage has no special facilities, just experience gained over two decades of working with the cars, and trite though it might sound, the professionalism to do the work properly. This attitude is extremely important in terms of maintaining the shape and getting an accurate finish to the cars. Edwards believes that the Interceptor shape in particular is a subtle thing, something which cannot always be readily appreciated by the casual observer. He maintains that by comparison, the slab-sided British or American cars are simple to work on. His view is that tolerances are large, and that some garages get away with fitting panels half-an-inch out here or there without it making much difference, and nobody really notices. But with all the extra double curves and movements of panels that there are on the Italian bodies, anything half-an-inch out looks a different car to a trained eye.

Seeing a car in build at the Jensen works, it is obvious that it is a slow and laborious process. It is evident from the way that the innermost box sections are built up on the

chassis that unless some sort of protective coat is sprayed right into them, there is a strong possibility of corrosion setting in at some point in the car's life. Edwards sees this as the legacy of an Italian design tradition. They design a car with a beautifully styled body, and some other poor sucker will have to sort out all the problems of manufacturing, and turn it into something that is going to last.

In his experience, all Italian cars rust in temperate climates and, of course, the manufacturer has to reach a compromise between his own production methods, practicalities of the car's design, and what the customer will pay for the finished product. In common with a lot of 'hand-made' cars, the Interceptor's character and to some extent its vulnerability lies in its build process. And if it is literally assembled by hand, it is a repeat process when the time comes to rebuild or restore it. Says Edwards:

You can throw the clock out of the window. When contemplating a rebuild, you have to realize that it is going to be a long and expensive process. To start with, nothing fits. It never did fit when they made it. They have never been able to afford the sort of tooling expenses necessary for every panel anyway, so Jensen manufacture has always been a sort of sub-assembly job. They made the chassis up to drawings with a tape measure and every one would be slightly different. This applies to the panels as well. They were tooled up fairly cheaply too, crude pressings that were just pop-riveted, not spot-welded together, and they had to be made to fit. Then the builder had to create the shape of the car within the making of those panels as well. Cutting, closing, lead-loading, reshaping. A veritable work of art.

When a restorer tackles the front end of a car, including both front wings and front panel, if he is very brave or very experienced then he will remove all three sections and

A *fully restored Interceptor Convertible ready for the road at the Jensen factory.*

There are usually between twenty or thirty cars in the throes of restoration at the factory; the couple in the foreground are completed.

Wood-veneer door trims of the prototype are probably shared with only one other Interceptor.

Badge of the flourishing Jensen Owners' Club.

put three new ones on. However, it is more prudent to do one at a time, because straight from the factory press none of them fit each other. Sometimes wings are as much as an inch too long. The solution is not down to lead-loading; it is hacking it about, and still making it look like a proper wing. During one memorable restoration, Cropredy Bridge Garage got through five sets of front panels and wings before they found any that they could actually use to complete the job, without it taking an age to fiddle with.

However, Edwards is far from scathing of factory methods. Far from it, for he well understands the problems. There is no way they can be expected to produce better panels because they are still using the original tooling. Cropredy have been at it long enough to be able to produce their own panels as well and, in theory, they could manufacture a brand-new Interceptor. As Edwards says, that is not part of their function, since the factory has many more resources to call on and, in any case, there just isn't enough demand for the car.

But with the panels which they do make, Cropredy do have similar problems to the factory, in that they don't fit either. These are the best panels they have ever used, and yet getting panels to fit has been a perennial problem for Jensen. It is the same for virtually all other hand-built cars. From

Specialists

With any specialized vehicle, or one with a particular following, the best place to find one if you're a cash buyer, or a new owner in need of maintenance, is through the Owners' Club. In the UK, Jensen owners are indeed well served, for the Club secretary is well-known authority Keith Anderson, author of the recent excellent history of the company, and editor of the *Jensen Owners' Club Magazine*. US owners have their own magazine *The White Lady* which is equally well produced, informative and packed with picture of club meets. There are always a few cars for sale in these magazines, and the classified columns of the classic car mags yield one or two Interceptors a month. If you're uncertain of what to look for when buying an Interceptor, it's a good idea to go to a specialist dealer. Cropredy Bridge Garage (029575 8444) always has a selection available, as does Steven Mee at 'Exclusively Jensen' (05436 84810) at Burntwood near Lichfield; in 1991 he was offering the very first two FFs, fully restored for £26,000 each, as well as the factory prototype Interceptor SP. Sturdy and Lowe (0226 713909) of Grimethorpe, Barnsley, specialize in complete mechanical and bodywork restorations. There are several other specialists who advertise in the *Jensen Owners' Club Magazine*, and Keith Anderson's address is 40 Hereford Way, Banbury, Oxon OX16 7RH.

1 Roof panel assy	centre	connection RH	LH
2 Crossmember – front – roof panel	11 Panel – rear quarter RH	20 Panel – stoneguard connection LH	28 Stiffener – screen pillar RH
3 Crossmember – rear – roof panel	12 Panel – rear quarter LH	21 Panel – rear quarter – upper – inner RH	29 Stiffener – screen pillar LH
4 Reinforcement – boot hinge RH	13 Stoneguard – rear RH	22 Panel – rear quarter – upper – inner LH	30 Panel – scuttle top assy
5 Reinforcement – boot hinge LH	14 Stoneguard – rear LH	23 'B' post upper assy RH	31 Reinforcement – lock mtg.
6 Cantrail RH – roof panel	15 Rear pillar assy RH	24 'B' post upper assy LH	32 Locating plate – lock mtg. bracket
7 Cantrail LH – roof panel	16 Rear pillar assy LH	25 Panel – boot skirt – inner	33 Support panel – boot – centre
8 Boot-lid frame assy – unpainted	17 Panel – rear quarter – inner – lower RH	26 Windscreen pillar RH	34 Rail RH – boot clearance
9 Panel – rear parcel shelf	18 Panel – rear quarter – inner – lower LH	27 Windscreen pillar	35 Rail LH – boot clearance
10 Panel – rear –	19 Panel – stoneguard		36 Bump rubber – axle tunnel

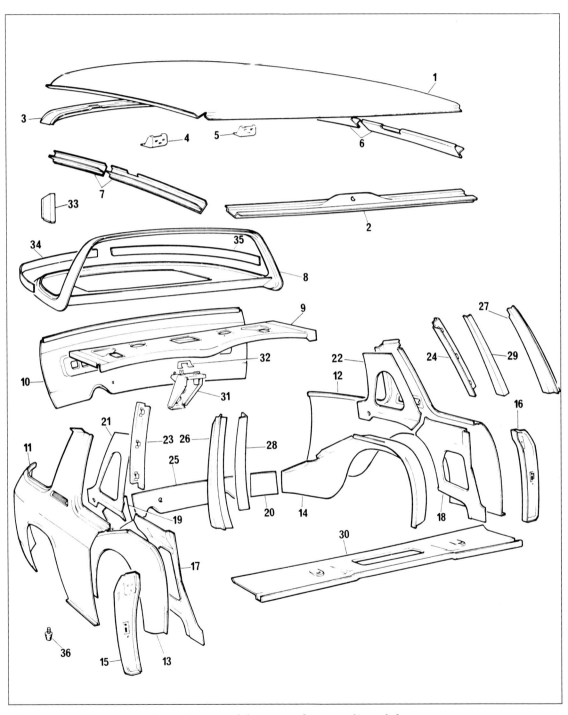

The panels which go to make up the rear of the car are less complicated than the front, since there are fewer mechanical components to incorporate. The factory keeps a number of the larger pressings in stock.

Aston Martins and Bristols to Facel Vegas and Rolls Royces, they were all the same. Edwards hints at stories of Rolls Royce's having to fly fitters out to foreign parts to fit wings on cars for distant dealerships because their own people just refused to do it. It isn't widely realized that the manufacturing process for such prestigious vehicles is relatively crude, with a great deal of making good being an integral part of that process. Edwards's main problem is selling that to the customer – who may have just been charged £200 for having a new wing fitted on the family hack Metro – getting him to understand why it is going to cost him perhaps £2,000 to have a similar job done on his Interceptor. They still have trouble with insurance companes, convincing them that the man-hours they quote for are a reality.

Apart from making a lot of their own panels, Cropredy Bridge Garage carries a vast amount of stock for C-V8s and Interceptors, and will do what they can for 541s. They have just started producing Interceptor bumpers, but chrome plating is done elsewhere.

The best place to look for contacts if considering a Jensen restoration is in the *Jensen Owners' Club Magazine*. Some people specialize in one particular model, and other individuals are particularly good sources of spare parts. Sturdy and Lowe is a northern garage which has changed hands a few times since 1976, and is not getting back on the map; Slipstream Autos in north London have been progressing since leaving Folletts. But with regard to size of operation and business structure, Cropredy Bridge Garage is the leader. In 1995, Andrew Edwards sold the business to its current owner, Bob Cherry, a technician who served most of his apprenticeship with the Jensen Motor Company.

Index

174 · *Jensen Interceptor*